Inner Peace

Inner Peace

Using the Lord's Prayer in Contemplation

by Ron Sebring

CBP Press
St. Louis, Missouri

Copyright © 1990 CBP Press
All rights reserved. No part of this book may be reproduced without written permission from CBP Press, Box 179, St. Louis, MO 63166.

Unless otherwise indicated, scripture quotations are from the Revised Standard Version of the Bible, copyright 1946, 1952, © 1971, 1972 by the Division of Christian Education of the National Council of Churches of Christ in America and used by permission.

Excerpts marked JB are from the Jerusalem Bible, copyrighted © 1966, 1967, and 1968 by Dartman, Longman & Todd Ltd. and Doubleday & Company, Inc., and used by permission.

Library of Congress Cataloging-in-Publication Data

Sebring, Ron.
    Inner peace : using the Lord's prayer in contemplation / Ron Sebring.
    136 p.
    ISBN 0-8272-1608-4 : $9.95
    1. Lord's prayer.   2. Prayer.   3. Contemplation.   I. Title
BV230.S382   1990
248.3'2—dc20   89-27523
                                                                                                 CIP

Printed in the United States of America

Contents

Introduction 7

Part I: The Nature and Methods of Prayer
   1. The Nature of Prayer and the Quest for Inner Peace ... 15
   2. Five Principal Conditions of Prayer 25
   3. The Spiritual Stance for Prayer 39

Part II: Praying the Lord's Prayer
   4. The Inner Structure of the Lord's Prayer 49
   5. The Imperative Tone of the Lord's Prayer 55
   6. The Corporate Nature of the Lord's Prayer 59
   7. The Personal Relationship of the Lord's Prayer 65
   8. The Transcendent Dimension of the Lord's Prayer 69
   9. The Hallowing of God's Name 73
  10. The Fullness of God's Kingdom 79
  11. Yielding to God's Will 83
  12. Our Daily Substance 89
  13. The Immediacy of Life 93
  14. Our Forgiven State 99
  15. The Necessity of Forgiving Others 107
  16. Life's Testings 117
  17. Overcoming the Fundamental Human Flaws 123
  18. The Context of the Lord's Prayer 129

Conclusion 133

Prayer, contemplative and discursive,
is the fundamental focus of religious life.

If prayer falters,
religion becomes mechanical.

If prayer succeeds,
religion becomes the greatest joy.

This book is dedicated to the dream
that one day
there will be peace on earth
and good will among all people.

The key to world peace lies in
a widespread sense of inner peace
 among world citizens.

To a world rife with conflict,
for individuals racked with stress,
this book offers several ways to pray
and suggests the resources
that can be expected from prayer
as revealed in the Lord's Prayer.

Introduction

One day I discovered a secluded rock overlooking an old fishing lake. It was a comfortable place to sit and offered a spectacular view of a cove seldom visited by people. It was a perfect spot for reflection.

That was early in my ministry, when I was a young and inexperienced pastor of a small Midwestern congregation. Now, years later, the rock and others like it have become holy ground. The grass nearby has been watered with my tears and is both green from the liquid and brown from the salt. Trees and birds singing in the branches have been my teachers. Fish nibbling at the surface and frogs on lily pads have been my counselors.

There have been times in my life when I honestly did not know how I would cope except for the quiet moments I spent on rocks beside lake waters. The issues of real life and the ideals of Christianity—forgiveness, faith, love—seemed poles apart. During those quiet times, through prayer and contemplation, I discovered a quality of inner peace that has merged the concrete experiences of life with the principles of Christian faith, principles that before were mere abstractions.

Christians are overwhelmed with information *about* faith, so much so that they believe religion is something learned rather than experienced. The more Bible they quote, the more information they assimilate, the more they can maintain the illusion of being religious.

Consequently, religion in western culture tends to be more a head trip and less a journey of the heart. This seems true in every quarter. Bible groups sit in folding chairs *discussing* passages of scripture. Ministers stand behind pulpits *expounding* tenets of faith. Seminary students gather in classrooms to stir in a soup of "ics" and "ologies"—theology, ethics, Christology, hermeneutics, anthropology, homiletics, soteriology, eschatology, ecclesiology, etc. Religion can become so much a play on words that the faith undergirding it appears to be more of a reflection about God than a direct experience of God.

So how is religion *experienced*?

Many activities compete for a Christian's allegiance, passing for the *experience* of religion: attending church regularly, tithing one's income, reading the Bible, doing good service, obeying the commandments. Silent injunctions shout: Do these things and you will be religious. Go through these motions and you will be practicing Christianity. Believe these creeds and you will experience God.

Yet people can read books on Christianity and send checks to favorite charities and still be hostile toward others. They can file out of their favorite places of worship, Bibles under arms, and still feel empty inside. By all social standards they are religious. But their inner worlds can remain poisoned with spiritual pollutants: pride, idolatry, guilt, resentment, worry, and depression. The inner peace accessible through Christian faith eludes them.

I have known committed Christians who were unable to make their faith work during the critical moments in their lives. Why? While becoming informed about the Bible and practicing the outer manifestations of Christianity, they never mastered its inner significance.

I have come to believe that only through prayer, the fundamental practice of Christianity, does religion develop depth. Prayer offers the necessary means of experiencing God by providing contact with that holy and tranquil center around which all events rotate. All outward manifestations of Christianity, whether expressions of love or moral perfection, are the natural results of experiencing the inner reality of God. All blessings, whether healing, prosperity, the realization of joy, or the resolution of difficult situations, are encouraged by prayer.

While prayer is spontaneous, it is also a learned skill. The stronger and more practiced the craft, the richer and more meaningful the experience. The purpose of this book is to provide a practical manual for developing prayer skills. With such skills one is free to explore uncharted spiritual realms and to discover the treasures buried therein.

Admittedly, this intent is crippled by offering a "head trip" for what is essentially a journey of the heart. However, every skill has both a theoretical and a practical side. While the latter is the doing, the former is reflecting on how it is done. Each side informs the other, and though practice precedes theory, if one is ignored in favor of the other, the results are less than what they might be.

Consider two people who want to learn music. One checks out books from the library and studies music theory. The other curls eager fingers over a keyboard and begins playing. Though one will understand the subject and the other will develop an ear for sound, neither will master the craft. Only as an individual applies practiced techniques to the instrument will musical skill develop.

Prayer is a skill that develops in the same way. One can study the Bible and read books about prayer, gathering much knowledge. If one does not pray, however, this means nothing. On the other hand, one can venture forth into life, praying only in a crisis or when something is desired. Though such prayers may be meaningful, the richness of a fully developed Christian life is lacking.

This book will examine the ways and means of prayer, the "how to" and "what for," the procedures for praying and the resources one can expect from the continued and concentrated practice of prayer.

Part one will examine theology and methodology, offering an understanding of prayer and an examination of what makes it work. Several details, simple things, foster the depth of prayer, while other things, subtle and deceptive, hinder the experience.

Part two will explore the resources of prayer. The abundant supply of spiritual resources available through prayer is clearly set forth in the Lord's Prayer. If one prays the Lord's Prayer, savoring every word and phrase, one will find everything necessary for a complete and balanced spiritual life. The Lord's Prayer is the whole recipe for spiritual growth. All the ingredients for inner peace are contained therein.

Three observations are worth noting in regard to the subject and scope of this book. First, any spiritual journey is spurred forward when we recognize its value. Before prayer will be effective, you must sense its importance, hungering for the peace it can give. Once you smell the aroma of sanctity and taste its goodness, you will develop a craving for it.

Many of the parables of Jesus have as their sole point the importance of recognizing value. A man discovered a treasure in a field and sold all he had to purchase the field. A merchant found a pearl of great worth and sold all he had to own the pearl.

Second, the concept of prayer assumed in the following pages is admittedly limited. Prayer is here considered as an activity to be done from time to time. For those mature in faith, there is a sense in which prayer is a perpetual activity. True saints experience all life as prayer. For them, the spirit of prayer embraces the whole context of living. There is no place where prayer stops and the rest of life begins. For such people, this book may seem to advocate part-time spirituality.

Praying without ceasing, however, is possible only for those mature in faith. Most people, even long-time Christians, have yet to reach the level of spiritual perfection at which they experience perpetual communion with God. The awareness of God easily slips away when the concerns of the world bear down.

This book will emphasize prayer in its more traditional forms, that is, concerted efforts to address God and/or to be open to hear God's speaking to us. It is through such efforts, practiced over time, that one gains the ability to pray without ceasing.

A third observation concerns a word of caution. Throughout this book, inner peace is understood as a tangible and verifiable experience, complete with calmness in the brain, relaxation in the muscles, and a slowed respiration and heart rate.

When Jesus hung on the cross—blood trickling down his cheeks and spikes burning in his hands—inner peace as described here certainly was not his experience. When we feel pain, frustration, and despair, it does not mean the kingdom of God has left us. People do not feel inner peace all the time.

In this book, setting such a concrete standard for inner peace and outlining specific ways of getting from here to there sometimes approaches the "self-help" heresy. The reader needs to take care not to step over the line. This can happen (1) when a person comes to believe that inner peace is something gained by personal effort rather than a gift from God, and (2) when he or she falls into self reproach because prayer doesn't seem to work. The tendency will be not to fault prayer or a book such as this that describes techniques for prayer but to blame oneself, to ask what is wrong with me that I can't make it work.

Herein lies the dilemma of any self-help approach. It creates the illusion that people are indeed helping themselves, and they either succeed or fail in that effort. Our society endorses self-help by nurturing the unexamined assumption that, if we follow the yellow brick road far enough and remain diligent, we will eventually reach Oz and all our questions will be answered. We little realize that all "wizards" are fake.

The techniques in this book are intended to enable people to wait for the God who runs to meet them. It is critically important to make the distinction between applying techniques in some kind of spiritual self-help program and practicing simple ways of being open to God.

The essence of prayer and contemplation is waiting. If we wait, empty and hopeful, truth comes to us. It's not something we embrace. It's something we allow to embrace us. We don't reach. We yield.

This is a "how to" book on waiting. It does not describe how to do something or how to get somewhere. Rather, it depicts how *not* to do something, how *not* to get in your own way. It describes how to create an open, receptive attitude so that communion with God can occur. It shows how to maintain this attitude while waiting.

There are times in life when people lose their sense of quietude, and this is OK. To pass through valleys of death's shadow and not become stuck, people sometimes must enter into feelings of despair.

There have been times in my own life when I have felt forsaken by God and techniques such as those described in this book have not worked. Sometimes I have given myself permission not to pray. At other times I have entered prayer, driven by a reckless intensity that abhors techniques, and I have experienced such prayers as beneficial. There have been times when I have prayed with no apparent results and have persisted until something broke through. Often situations changed. Equally as often, it was my perspective that changed. Almost always, in one way or another, prayer worked.

The regular practice of quiet prayer during the easy times hones the skills necessary for the more difficult moments. An image that captures this truth for me is the sun hiding behind clouds. Having experienced the brilliance of God's presence in moments of inner peace, we can enter the valleys of despair, even when clouds hide the sun and all attention is directed to navigating the terrain. God's glory still shines above the clouds, and the day will come when it is again possible to bask in its warmth. The kingdom of God is still present, even when we are less aware of it.

If communion with God becomes the single most important goal in your life, prayer will be your number one priority. The times you spend in prayer will be the most natural, most precious, most joy-filled moments of your day.

I recommend that you begin today, if you have not done so already, a regular, daily practice of prayer. Set aside a short block of time, preferably the same time each day. Find a secluded spot, a place that may become for you what my rocks beside lake waters have been for me. Take a moment to relax physically, and then pray.

I recommend that you move slowly through this book, allowing time to integrate whatever insights you glean about your prayer life. Food digests better when thoroughly chewed. So, too, insights are "digested" by observing how they apply and verifying them in experience.

As you become committed to a regular practice of prayer, your spirit will evolve toward the perfection of sainthood, or sanctification, which is the ultimate goal of Christianity. A pervasive and profound sense of inner peace will be the hallmark of your progress.

My sincere hope is that this book will make some contribution toward your journey.

Part I: The Nature and Methods of Prayer

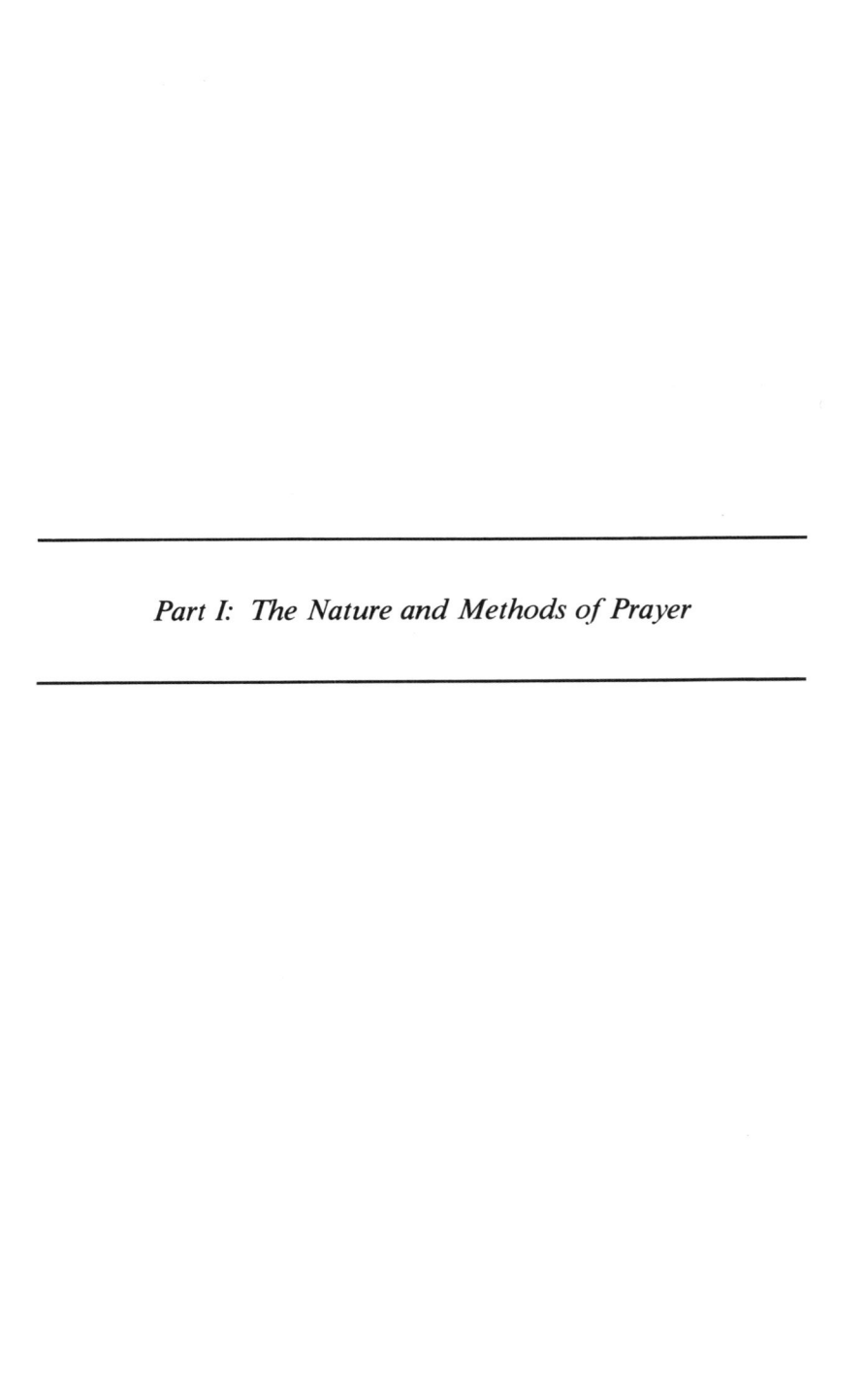

1. The Nature of Prayer and the Quest for Inner Peace

What makes people happy? For some, wealth is thought to hold the key. For others, pleasure and the enjoyment of life promises the most. Many seek happiness in knowledge, immersing themselves in various fields of study. Others pursue notoriety and acclaim. Benevolent service, doing good for others, is often hailed as the final good for human effort.

This book makes two assumptions. First, underneath it all, true happiness can be found only in inner peace. It is the ultimate quest of all persons and the hidden thirst of every soul. Second, inner peace is found through prayer, whether it be contemplative or discursive.

The Varieties of Prayer

People pray in many ways. Indeed the variety of ways it is done creates one of the difficulties for understanding prayer. Some pray spontaneously. They get up in the morning, pour their coffee, eat breakfast, drive to work, all the time talking with God as they would to a companion sitting next to them.

Others are meticulous about form. Open a liturgical book on prayer, and you are likely to find an outline such as: salutation, praise, confession, intercession, supplication, benediction. Many fine prayers have been spoken and written accordingly, and with little sacrifice in passion and integrity.

Different traditions hold separate assumptions about prayer. Protestants generally believe prayer is a direct exchange between the individual and God. Catholics, on the other hand, often employ a mediator such as a priest or a heavenly figure (a saint or the Virgin Mary).

Some pray discursively, packing a string of words between the parentheses of a "Dear Lord" and an "Amen." Others understand prayer as contemplation or meditation, focusing on a symbol or a sacrament or settling into silence to become aware of God's presence.

Turning to the Bible for a more definitive understanding of prayer only broadens the issue, for it contains several approaches. In many places, especially in the Old Testament, people conversed with God directly. Adam, Noah, Abraham, and Moses all had two-way conversations with God. Abraham even won an argument with God.

In other places, people communicated with God through dreams and visions. Jacob's ladder, Ezekiel's wheels in the middle of wheels, and Daniel's statue with clay feet, all represent metaphorical approaches to divine truth. At least six times in the birth stories of Jesus, God's message through dreams altered the course of events.

Communication with God sometimes meant reading the signs of the times. People felt God's will could be read in the way things happened: through famine, earthquake, war, Gideon wringing water from his fleece, a group of Israelites huddled in a circle to cast lots.

This method became sophisticated during the time of the prophets, when prayer meant recollection, that is, reviewing God's interventions in history and interpreting the implications for the people of the day.

In many places in the Bible, particularly in the Psalms, prayers were liturgical. They were written out, memorized, and repeated regularly, sometimes at established times during the day and sometimes on ceremonial occasions.

In contemporary practice and from the biblical witness, prayer is understood and practiced in a variety of ways. All style held in common the concerted effort to communicate with God and God's tireless and creative efforts to communicate with people. What the variety of approaches means is that there is no one acceptable way to pray. Each person and community of faith can experiment and find their special way of establishing communion with God.

When Prayer is Misused

Effective prayer depends not as much on how it is understood as on whether it is misunderstood. Distortions and false assumptions about prayer create the potential for futility.

Several years ago, a network newscast brought a report from a small Midwestern town caught in the worst drought in anyone's memory. The corn crop, the staple of economic life, was nearly destroyed. The people in this Bible-Belt community filed into their churches to pray for rain. They specified the day when the rains were to come.

The television camera focused over the heads of the congregation on a minister behind the pulpit. "After all," he said, quoting Mark 11:23–24, "Whoever says to this mountain, 'Be taken up and cast into the sea,' and does not doubt in his heart . . . it will be done for him. Therefore I tell you, whatever you ask in prayer, believe that you have received it, and it will be yours."

People interviewed after the service showed an unshakable belief that God would answer their prayer. On the morning of the specified day, the cameras were there, first showing a cloudless sky, then dropping below the trees to reveal a parched field with dwarfed stalks of corn three-fourths brown from the heat.

What went wrong?

A fundamental and universal error in prayer is assuming God's will happens to be the same as our own, or that with enough praying we can mold God's will to the shape of our own.

This is, in effect, playing God and is the common denominator of all sin. Imagine the glory people would claim if they could make it rain by uttering the words, "Please God, make it rain." Such a view of deity reduces God to a push-button computer that puts out what is fed into it.

Mixed with prayer, playing God becomes a dangerous and subtle form of sin. It is clothed in religious custom and therefore "seems" right. Who would point an accusing finger at someone on his or her knees, suggesting that something sinful is taking place? And it is dangerous because of the potential for oppression when people believe their whims express God's will. Some of the worst atrocities in history have been committed in the name of the kingdom of God.

Prayer so misunderstood leads to several abuses. Sometimes people treat prayer as a means of securing blessings. Prayer can indeed yield blessings—health, prosperity, social success—and it is certainly appropriate to ask for these things. However, the perspective of Jesus in the garden must ride as an appendage to all requests: "not my will, but thine be done" (Luke 22:44).

People in crises often pray for help, which is also appropriate. This becomes an abuse of prayer when they seek to tie God's will to specific results. For example, sometimes people try to make a deal with God, praying in effect, "God, if you pull me through this one, I'll get religious and attend church for the rest of my life," or "God, if you give me what I want, I'll try my best to be good. I'll stop doing such-and-such." In the garden, Jesus didn't get what he prayed for. God answered his prayer, not by removing the cross from him, but by giving him the strength to go through with it.

Sometimes people avoid responsibility by praying. They drop to their knees and pray for something, then do nothing, leaving it all to God. This allows the illusion that God's will has entered the situation while making no demands that they change their behavior. Prayer augments human effort. It is never a substitute for human effort. As the sailor once said, "It's good to trust in God, but secure your boat to the moorings."

People often ask others to pray for them, and this is appropriate. While intercessory prayer (praying on someone's behalf) has its place, it is never a substitute for personal effort. Sole reliance on others—a priest or minister, an elder or a supportive friend—represents an abuse of prayer because it tends to make one spiritually inarticulate. Spiritual health depends on cultivating one's own devotional life, and this means searching for ways in which one can mold one's will to God's.

Another abuse of prayer is burying it in public ritual. This is an expression of self-will in which one sinks into a feeling of complacency, believing that one's own dues to religion have been paid. In the culture in which Jesus lived, prayer was highly ritualized. Three times a day, when the temple bells tolled, people were expected to stop what they were doing and pray. The Pharisees—accidentally, on purpose—happened to be on the street corners of the market places when the bells rang. They shuffled their robes and bowed their heads in full view of everyone. Jesus called this pretense into question (Matt. 6) and taught that prayer is a personal, private matter and is something to be done behind the doors of one's closet.

In today's world, prayer enjoys many public forums—before meals, public meetings, even ball games. The right to pray in public schools is a hotly contested political issue. Such social rituals may, to a degree, participate in the true nature of prayer and are thus meaningful. However, they are not to be confused with the deeply personal and intrinsically private experience of prayer that Jesus so passionately taught and practiced.

What Is Prayer?

Though the New Testament was written in Greek, Jesus spoke Aramaic, and it is fair to assume that his message took shape in this language. The Aramaic word for prayer is built on the root meaning "to lay a trap." The metaphor suggests that prayer is mentally laying a trap, then waiting to snare the impulses and insights of God that are constantly moving below the surface of consciousness.

When I was in San Francisco, a friend took me crab fishing on a dock just under the Golden Gate bridge. He secured a piece of meat in the center of a wire cage designed to lay flat on the ocean floor. The cage was fastened to a rope that, when pulled, folded up the sides and captured the crabs that ventured onto it to devour the meat.

My friend hurled the trap out over the water, and we watched as it disappeared below the surface. It was dusk. I remember the awe I felt as I waited, staring at the rope that wound its way into the depths of a mysterious world about which I knew little.

After several minutes, and with no clues whether something had crawled into the trap, my friend pulled it to the surface. More often than not, there were crabs in the cage, and a few were keepers.

Prayer is like this. We are not trying to spear divine truth or wrestle it into being. We simply lay a trap in the silent and mysterious depths of our inner universe. Then we patiently wait, hoping to draw to the surface of consciousness some spiritual food that will nourish our lives and make us whole. The trap is our silence, or the words and visualization of the things we hope for. These draw unto themselves the subtle vibrations of God's unbounded energy, forming the divine food we draw up to consciousness and possible manifest in reality. Sometimes this food comes to us in symbolic form (dreams, visions, omens). Sometimes it comes in an enveloping sense of God's presence that somehow transcends all the words we can conjure to explain it. Sometimes it appears as unexpected blessings (prosperity, healing, harmonious relationships). And sometimes, we realize it in our intuitions regarding particular directions for our lives.

Of course, the ego can pollute all these things. Still, in the highest sense, apart from the ego-centered, self-willed approach people often take to it, *prayer is conscious communion with God*, whether it is we who take the steps to become aware of God or God who breaks into our consciousness.

All styles of prayer have as their goal the two-way connection between the surface of life and the depths of being, thus realizing the sense of oneness we have with God. Atonement (at-one-ment) is this oneness. Inner peace and the resultant state of outer harmony within the communities in which we live are the by-products of this divine-human unity.

Conscious *Communion* with God

Prayer is communication with God, but this is only the beginning. The words "communication" and "communion," as well as "community," have as their root the word "common." Communication happens when people reach a *common* understanding. Community happens when a group of people, sharing something in *common*, gather in one place. In worship, communion (common-union) happens when people, while sharing a *common* sacrament, experience their unity with one another in a *common* faith.

Likewise, prayer as conscious communion with God happens when we experience our commonness or unity with God, whether it be with words or visualizations or simply through being immersed in the silence within, listening. The spark of divinity that is the essence of each of us resonates with the creative source of all reality.

Conscious Communion with God

There is a sense in which our unity with God is already the reality. Everything lives and moves and has its being in God.

Sin is separation from God. People experience problems precisely because they are unconscious of God; that is, they become oblivious to anything beyond the babble of their own egos. Two biblical metaphors for this are "sleep" and "death." Normally, people live as if in a dream-like trance, spiritually dead. These images will be explored in greater detail later.

Prayer means bringing the reality of our innate oneness with God into consciousness. We are no longer separated from God. We are one with God, and thus able to let go and let God govern our lives. This means allowing God's will to flow in and through us.

Conscious Communion *with God*

Prayer is compromised when one does not have a functional understanding of deity. To fully appreciate prayer as conscious communion with God, we must examine the concept of God. People pray according to the way they understand God.

When the question is asked, "What is God like?" answers range from cryptic definitions like "God is spirit" to childlike images of "an old man with a robe and a long white beard sitting on a throne in heaven."

Philosophers discuss God in terms of God's attributes: omnipresence, omniscience, omnipotence. God is everywhere; God is all-knowing; God is all-powerful. Such definitions duck the real issues. *What* is everywhere? *Who* is all-knowing? *What* is all-powerful?

In popular language, God is personified with anthropomorphic poetry. For example, God is a male person with eyes that watch us and ears that hear what we say. He is angry or is pleased. He walks with people in gardens, talks with people in places of worship, and carries people across beaches leaving only one set of footprints. Sometimes he sends good fortune, and sometimes he strikes with proverbial "lightning bolts." Though people often outgrow the literalness of these images, they seldom replace them.

The biggest problem with cryptic, philosophic, or popular anthropomorphic notions of deity, so far as prayer is concerned, is that they leave us feeling distant from God. God is felt to be out there, other than who we are. If God is a cosmic Santa Claus, bestowing blessing according to who is naughty or nice, or a universal Judge, separating the innocent from the guilty and measuring out punishment accordingly, or a celestial Peeping Tom, watching our every thought and move, then prayer carries the heavy burden of having to placate God. We must perform, defend our case, or evade detection.

Understanding prayer as conscious communion with God requires a mature concept of the divine, one that pictures deity as imminent as well as transcendent, a presence closer to us than we are to ourselves. Then prayer becomes, not a way of bridging distance, but a way of removing blinders.

Several years ago I had a conversation with an avowed atheist. "I do not believe in God," she said. I asked her to describe the God she did not believe in. After all, to deny something we must have a conception of what is denied. With some thought, she explained that she could not believe in a supreme being, off in the sky somewhere, intervening in people's lives. I agreed with her conclusions. I, too, do not believe in that kind of God. Such a God, no matter how supreme, is separate or distinct from other beings. Such a God would "act upon" creation as opposed to "acting in" creation—or, maybe better—as opposed to forming the intelligent context within which creation acts.

My friend and I discussed alternative views. What we concluded, and what still makes sense to me, is understanding God as Divine Intelligence, the *Logos* or Creative Wisdom and Sustaining Force that undergirds the universe. (It would be nice if our language would allow these things to be represented as verbs instead of nouns.)

Admittedly, these images constitute more anthropomorphisms. They conceive God in terms of human attributes—mind or consciousness. However, for me, they address the reality of God in a meaningful way, enabling both an immanent and a transcendent sense of God's presence.

Consider the metaphor of a pond teeming with life. Due to human negligence, pollutants enter the waters and the ecology of the pond is severely damaged. Fish and vegetation begin to die. After a time, the error is discovered and the pollution is stopped. The pond is left alone and slowly revives. Some force or guiding intelligence transcendent to each fish, snail, or patch of moss in the pond and at the same time immanent within the pond itself knows how to adjust the ecology of the pond. It is as if everything in the pond lives and moves and has its being *in* this Guiding Intelligence that simultaneously is *in* everything in the pond.

On a cosmic scale, Divine Intelligence is that which orchestrates reality. This immanence is what makes a personal relationship with God possible, as opposed to beliefs that assume God's distance—the "great architect" of masonry or the "divine watchmaker" of eighteenth century deism. Such views, which still linger today, picture God as creating the world and then standing apart from it, watching it run and intervening at appropriate moments to "fix" things.

The primary reason people are normally unaware of the God within is that their senses are oriented outward, toward the manifest world. When we look within, we avail ourselves of the opportunity to become aware of God as a living, indwelling presence.

Prayer is conscious communion with the indwelling God. It is becoming one with the Universal Creative Consciousness in which we live and move and have our being.

The difference between one who prays and one who does not is that the latter is tossed about by events, with no sense of purpose or meaning, like a piece of debris caught in the ocean currents. He or she has no direction but is rather a victim of what happens. One who prays, thus attaining to the presence of God, is better able to understand the flow of divine will and knows how to navigate the currents.

Sensing God's presence is a fleeting experience, constantly threatened by the concerns of the world. Hence, our communion with God must be renewed. Prayer is the exercise that keeps us in spiritual shape by strengthening our sense of unity with God. Like any exercise, its effectiveness depends on its regularity. Constantly, Jesus felt the need to retreat to private places and to reclaim the sense of unity with God through prayer.

One prays for the sake of prayer itself and not for what can be gained in the manifest world. As was mentioned earlier, gains do come through prayer, whether healing, prosperity, or changes in difficult situations. These things, however, are best understood as by-products of a true communion with God.

Regular prayer does make a difference in people's lives. Once I knew a man who had an unusual countenance. Whether standing or walking, he was relaxed and at ease. His voice was soft, yet it projected great force. He seldom spoke, but when he did, his words were perfectly timed and targeted to the situation.

On one occasion, I watched him enter a room where there was intense conflict. His mere presence had a calming effect. When the discussion stopped and faces turned to him, beckoning for his opinion, his comments settled the dispute.

This man was a committed Christian, but he had something many Christians lack. Wanting to know his secret, I visited his home and discovered his habit of going into a special room he had constructed. It was an elaborate private chapel with a carpeted floor, large pillows, candles, incense on a homemade altar, and sacred pictures on the wall. The room was used solely for prayer. It was a private sanctuary that he visited often, mostly early in the morning and late in the evening. Sometimes he entered the chapel to read devotional material, sometimes to articulate a prayer, and to sometimes just sit.

Since visiting this man I have discovered others with the same qualities—a marked sense of inner peace and the ability to project it, enabling harmony in their relationships. They also had a special place to which they regularly retreated to pray. One woman who lived on a farm told of going to a spot beside a creek at the far end of the pasture. Even in cold weather she bundled up and made her way to the creek. most of the time to pray but sometimes just to listen to the water gurgling beneath the ice.

In knowing these people and as a result of frequent visits to my rocks beside lake waters, I have come to believe that inner peace and a corresponding influence for outer harmony is the visible result of regular prayer. Inner peace, once obtained, is an individual's most precious possession. Nothing is as important. It is a pearl of great price, the kingdom of God within.

Inner peace and outer harmony, the secret longing and ultimate quest of every soul, is born and matures through the regular practice of prayer. In the following chapters, we will explore ways of establishing a communion with God and enjoying the resultant states of inner peace and outer harmony.

[handwritten: object for worship center]

[handwritten: object that symbolizes a pray concern]

2. Five Principal Conditions for Prayer

Prayer is like placing an arrow in a bow and taking aim. If the aim is off even a fraction of an inch, the target will be missed. On the other hand, if the arrow is placed where it will receive maximum thrust and if the aim is precise, all the archer needs to do is let go. If you establish the physical and mental context for prayer with this same precision, the results will be equally as automatic. The prayer flies automatically to God, a paradoxically still and moving target who perpetually seeks our aim.

Five conditions are critical for establishing the physical and mental context for prayer: (1) quiet, (2) stillness, (3) settled breathing, (4) physical and mental relaxation, and (5) a narrowed focus of concentration. If quiet, stillness, breath, relaxation, and focus are perfected with each prayer session, the depth of prayer will be enhanced. Over time, the accumulated effect will be a profound state of inner peace and a substantial influence for outer harmony.

Quiet

While driving through southern Missouri, I stopped for a tour of one of the caves. Not particularly interested in the guided tour, I found a corner where I could sit and experience simply being in the cave. The most enduring recollection of that moment was the profound quiet. The slightest sound was amplified—my heart beating, a drip in a pool several yards away, even my own thoughts. The quiet

[handwritten: Heb. 11:1A]

that engulfed these sounds was more than an emptiness, an absence of sound. It was noticeable, like the presence of something tangible and living. In that moment, I understood why Elijah and others in the Bible sought sanctuary in caves.

Experiencing the quiet of a cave reveals just how noisy and filled with commotion life really is. There is little wonder why stress takes such a toll in people's lives. Everyone literally hungers for quiet, for it is in quiet that health returns and energy is restored.

Quiet is a function of a subdued environment. The first condition for effective prayer is finding a personal sanctuary, a quiet place for periodic retreats.

What is a sanctuary? An animal sanctuary is a place where animals are not startled by the crack of a hunter's gun. A fugitive seeking sanctuary looks for a place beyond the range of sirens and the clinking of handcuffs. A prayer sanctuary is a place set aside where one can escape the commotion and confusion of the world—telephones and schedules and rush-hour traffic.

Throughout the scriptures people sought quiet sanctuaries, places within which they could retreat into silence and commune with God. When the early Hebrews camped, they built altars some distance from their tents, usually high on the hilltops. These were places to which they could retreat and pray. Samuel heard the voice of God while alone in the temple sanctuary. Elijah needed the sanctuary in a cave to reclaim his inner peace and sense of mission. Jesus constantly sought isolated places where he could be alone for prayer.

A prayer sanctuary is a quiet place where you can retreat and make your journey inward, unencumbered. It may be a secluded spot in the woods, a grassy meadow beside a stream, or a rock beside lake waters. It can be as elaborate as a chapel or as simple as a small closet or isolated corner. If outdoors, the sights and sounds of nature make an ideal setting for prayer. If indoors, you can enhance the atmosphere with subdued lighting and provisions for comfort (a pillow, candles, and maybe a kneeling rail). Some people burn incense. Others give attention to decor—traditional and personal symbols that remind them of God.

Jesus taught that prayer, being a private matter, is something to be done alone (Matt. 6:6). Constantly he left his disciples and the crowds for secluded places. This was the practice of great individuals throughout the Bible: Abraham, Moses, Samuel, Elijah, John the Baptist, Paul.

Prayer, of course, is possible at any moment. However, for real depth, a quiet and secluded place is indispensable. It is like a greenhouse within which spiritual growth thrives.

Stillness

All living things oscillate between stillness and motion, rest and activity. Indeed, this is the binary structure of all vibrations, all wavelike phenomena, which includes just about everything. Oriental philosophy understands this oscillation as the *yin* and *yang* of existence.

To live in the world necessitates motion. Earning a living, enjoying family and friends, participating in social causes, all require that we be active and attentive to the material world. Activity springs from disequilibrium; this means that, in some way, conflict is involved. Living is asserting the self against resistance to achieve a synthesis or renewed equilibrium. This is why life, whether we enjoy the process or not, can be exhausting. A simpler way to put it is to borrow the cliches of our day: no matter how you slice it, life is a rat race!

Our sanity depends on interspersed intervals of sleep, rest, and breaks in the continuum of activity. Indeed, life itself is an oscillation between stillness and motion, rest and activity.

It is important to understand that prayer is not an activity like the other things we do. It is more akin to the other end of the oscillation. It is a non-activity, a non-doing, like sleep, except that in prayer awareness is heightened. To pray, you must give up the need to be doing something and simply be present. As the psalm commands, "Be still and know that I am God" (Ps. 46:10). Prayer means stillness, and a by-product of prayer is rest.

How can stillness for prayer be achieved? While quiet is a function of a subdued environment, stillness is a function of a comfortable, stable, and upright posture.

The Bible gives some attention to the postures of prayer. Sometimes people stood with arms stretched toward heaven; sometimes they knelt; sometimes they lay prostrate on the ground.

Christian tradition also has concerned itself with posture, the classical position being the kneeling position with hands folded. Some denominations provide kneeling rails for prayer. Artists have incorporated the hand placement for prayer in their masterpieces. Children are pictured kneeling beside their beds at night, hands folded and heads bowed.

The most effective posture for prayer is a comfortable position with a stable base and vertical spine. These factors are important because they enable stillness and concentration. A stable, well-grounded base enables the body to become motionless and thus fosters a stillness of spirit. The mind is most alert when the spine is vertical. A reclined posture is associated with sleep and may lead to inattention.

A kneeling posture meets these conditions, and this may be the reason for its popularity through the centuries. You can also maintain a stable base with vertical spine while seated in a chair or on the floor with your legs crossed.

Once you assume a vertical and stable posture, find a comfortable position for your hands—folded in your lap, resting on your knees, cupped together in a variation of the classical "praying hands" position.

There is something subtle about a consistent hand position for prayer as indicated by the attention given to it throughout the centuries, not only in Christianity but in other religions as well. Over time, the mind associates the habitual position of the hands with prayer. When your mind has made this connection, simply assuming the hand position suggests the spirit of prayer.

Placing the tip of the tongue behind the upper front teeth, relaxing the jaw so the teeth are slightly separated, closing the eyes, allowing the forehead and cheeks to relax—all this enables a greater depth in prayer.

A lake cannot reflect the mountain range behind it as long as the wind is blowing. Only as the motion ceases, allowing the surface to become glassy smooth, does the reflection become flawless. It is so with prayer. Only as motion ceases and the body becomes still, allowing the mind to settle, do you experience your deepest self as the reflection of God within.

Settled Breathing

Psychologists have observed that disturbances in breathing rhythm accompany emotional patterns. Breath-holding, for example, indicates anxiety. Sudden inhalation is associated with surprise and fear. Marked exhalation suggests disgust. When the breathing pattern relaxes, a person is calm. If the breathing is not settled, a disturbance of some kind, positive or negative, is present. Breathing is thought to be the connecting link between the mind and the deeper realms of the spirit.

For centuries, monks and mystics have recognized the importance of a settled breathing pattern for prayer and meditation. In the stillness of breath they found the transcendent states of consciousness.

In the Bible, "breath" and "wind" are associated with "spirit." God breathed into Adam the spirit of life (Gen. 2:7). On Pentecost, the spirit of God descended as the wind (Acts 2:2).

The third condition for effective prayer is to allow the breathing to become *natural, even, slow,* and *deep.* After you have assumed an upright and stable posture in your prayer sanctuary, you can initiate the settling process by focusing your attention on your breathing, either at the nostrils where the air passes in and out or at the base of the abdomen where it expands and contracts with each breath. Then, simply follow your breathing with your awareness. Notice how it evens out, slows, and deepens.

An artificial but effective way to begin the settling process is to take a deep breath and hold it for several seconds. Then exhale, allowing your body to relax and the emotions to let go. This is something you do consciously, and is therefore unnatural. It is important, after doing this one or more times, that you relinquish all control of your breathing and simply watch the settling process.

Left alone, your breathing will settle naturally. When you have a goal, no matter how trivial, effort can slip in unconsciously. It is important that you not make your breathing settle but allow it to do so.

As the residue of emotional intensity from daily concerns relaxes, in and out motions become rhythmic, and breaths become evenly spaced. In a short time, the whole process slows. Each breath reaches deeper into the abdomen. During prayer, the breathing may periodically cease, a physical indicator of the depth of your prayer.

Once while driving up the coast of California, I stopped along a secluded beach to sit quietly and watch the waves licking against the shore. Each wave was unique, different in minute ways, and yet there was an uncanny uniformity in size and pattern. Life is like this. All events and all things, being wave-like, are rhythmic. Up and down, in and out, back and forth, collapse and expand, day and night, summer and winter—all creation waltzes to the Creator's drum beat.

The closest connection you and I have with this divine rhythm is our heartbeat and our breathing. By allowing your breath to settle— and you may notice that in the process your heartbeat will synchronize with your breathing—you are lulled into the spirit of prayer.

Physical and Mental Relaxation

The depth of your prayers is directly related to how thoroughly you relax, both mentally and physically. Tension hides in muscle groups throughout the body and is associated with the frustrations of daily life, with past events and unreconciled conflicts, and with anticipated future occurrences. These tense spots create an "uptight" feeling and steal energy vital for prayer. Releasing these tensions frees the spirit for communion with God and fosters a sense of inner peace.

Physical relaxation is a skill that can be learned. If you take time to master it, you will have an invaluable tool for augmenting prayer. On an occasion separate from prayer, you may wish to experiment with relaxation by lying on your back and systematically going over your body, starting with the legs. Tense and let go with each muscle group, in turn, throughout your body. By the time you finish, you will have entered a state of deep relaxation.

Another method for conditioning your body to relax is to assume a seated or reclined position. Focus on various parts of the body, suggesting to each part, in turn, to relax. As an example, you may focus on your right arm and think the word "relax." Feel your arm respond to the suggestion as the sensation of relaxation swells. Think the word "heavy" and feel the heaviness in your right arm. Imagine the sun shining on your right arm and feel it warm. Feel a gentle breeze blowing across the skin of your right arm and experience the coolness. With this method, start with the extremities and work inward. Finish by relaxing the tiny muscles about the spine.

Warm and heavy sensations are associated with relaxation. As muscles relax, blood rushes into the area and it literally warms. As tension leaves the muscles, you feel the weight of what the tension supported; hence, the heaviness. In learning to relax, notice these things.

Later, as your prayers mature and as your consciousness disassociates from your body, the heaviness may be replaced with a light, uplifting, walking-on-water feeling.

A third method for practicing relaxation uses visualization. One of the values of soothing imagery is that it relaxes the mind as well as the body, supplanting the thoughts and images connected to tensions with those associated with peace and harmony. While lying or seated in a comfortable position, imagine a peaceful setting. You might see yourself lying on a beach, listening to the surf and the gulls in the distance, and feeling the sun warm various parts of your body. Or you might picture yourself beside a stream in a wooded meadow, listening to the gurgling water, the birds in the trees, and feeling a cool breeze against your skin.

Each time you experience total relaxation, take a moment to appreciate the sensation. Also condition your mind to assume this feeling of relaxation any time you choose by taking a deep breath, holding it for a moment, and exhaling while thinking the word "relax." When so conditioned, you will be able to return to a state of relaxation simply by taking a deep breath, holding it for a moment, and exhaling while giving yourself the suggestion to relax.

Once you are familiar with how it feels to be relaxed and have conditioned yourself to relax at will, you can create a feeling of relaxation before you pray.

Relaxation is both physical and mental. Letting go of tensions in the body means letting go of the concerns that are creating these tensions. The mental counterpart to physical relaxation is surrendering, assuming a passive attitude. Such an attitude is crucial for effective prayer.

When I discuss with study groups the necessity of mental letting go, they often ask, "How?" The conversation usually turns to the topic of stress. While speaking of her troubles, one woman said, "I just can't stop thinking about them." Others complain about lying awake through the night, mulling over problems.

The command to "let go and let God" has been a boon to me. To instill a passive attitude, I have found it helpful to repeat this sentence over and over, until I feel its effect. It is a way of saying: whatever the problem, there is a higher power who will handle it, and though I will do my best, the outcome is ultimately in the hands of God, if I allow it.

Another statement that has given comfort to many comes from Rom. 8:28: "We know that in everything God works for good with those who love him, who are called according to his purpose." Believing that the outcome of whatever problem eventually works for good helps us let go and turn things over to God.

Letting go is a process that must be brought to consciousness. Unconsciously, it may never happen. When I was a youth on a vacation in Florida, friends taught me to water ski. They gave me the necessary instructions that enabled me to stand up for the first time. In my youthful arrogance, I tried to jump the wake on the outer edge of a turn and ended up doing a cartwheel over the top of the water. No one told me to let go of the rope. The next thing I knew, I was plowing through the water head first. It took several second before I consciously realized I would be better off letting go of the rope.

This is exactly how people cling to their problems. They hold them in an unconscious grip. To let go, the mind must sense the situation and search for the mechanisms that will release it. Sensing the problem, then reminding ourselves that God will ultimately handle it, enables us to "let go and let God."

Having entered your prayer sanctuary and assumed a comfortable posture, having allowed your breathing to settle, you should consciously let go, both physically and mentally. As described above, one way to relax physically is to take a breath, hold it for a few seconds, and exhale while thinking the word "relax." While exhaling the next breath, you can assume a passive and receptive attitude by repeating a phrase such as "let go and let God." Your mind and body will assume the attitude necessary for making prayer effective.

Narrowed and Sustained Focus of Concentration

Four states of consciousness are possible, depending on how tense or relaxed the body is and on how alert or dulled is the awareness. In deep sleep, the body is relaxed and awareness is dulled. In dream sleep, awareness is still entranced, but tensions associated with dreams enter the body. In a waking state, awareness rises to a higher level, while tensions from the stresses of life accumulate in the body. Normally, people experience only these three states of consciousness.

There exists a fourth state of consciousness qualitatively different from the other three. The brain waves are more alpha; the metabolic rate slows; the blood lactate level drops. This state of consciousness develops when the body is relaxed and awareness is concentrated. Relaxed alertness is the state of consciousness within which prayer is most effective.

If you have a tendency to sleep when you pray, your awareness is at the other end of the continuum. Since the relaxation necessary for prayer is conducive to sleep, it is important to take this fifth step and focus the range of awareness.

Awareness can be understood by comparing it to light. In our normal waking state, it is diffuse and spread out. We are marginally aware of many things. When we concentrate, it's like narrowing the beam to a spotlight that focuses on one particular thing. The more laser-like the awareness, the more heightened the concentration, and,

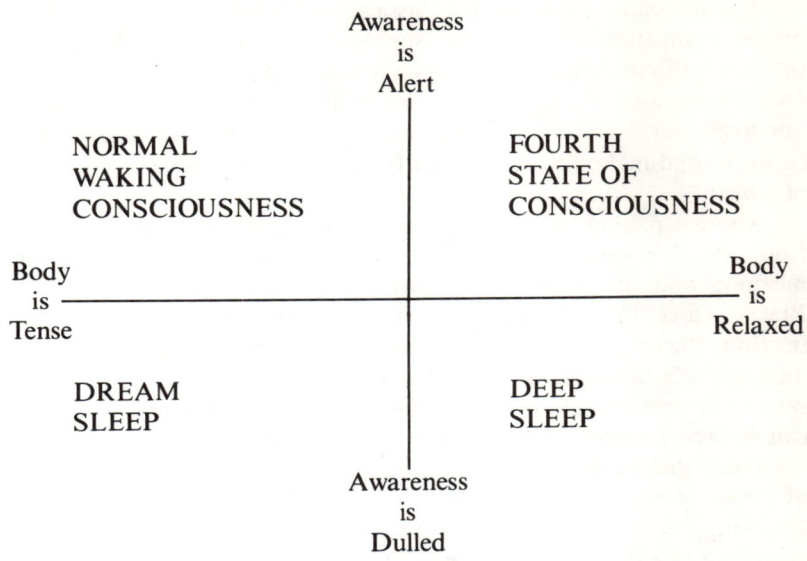

hence, the more intense the prayer will be. Remember: this intensity requires a relaxed body and a passive attitude.

What you focus on depends on what type of prayer you choose. Basically, there are two kinds: discursive and contemplative. Discursive prayer is talking to God; contemplative prayer is simply being in the presence of God.

Discursive Prayer

Discursive prayer formulates concerns in words, the most common form being a spontaneous conversing with God as one would with a friend.

There are other, more formal patterns. One prototype, employed by the prophets, follows a broad and loosely formatted structure consisting of a focus on (1) God's action in the past, (2) the current situation, and (3) future possibilities for divine intervention. This past-present-future flow provides both structure and spontaneity.

Another pattern is to use the classical outline for prayer: salutation, praise, confession, intercession, supplication, and benediction. The salutation (*Dear Lord*, for example) is followed by a spirit of thanksgiving. Such a spirit empowers the rest of the prayer. Next, we examine our lives, our problems, our human situation. Then we express our concerns and make our requests of God. Finally, we close in the name of Christ.

Another method of discursive prayer is to enter the intensity of the Lord's Prayer, saying each phrase in turn, concentrating on its full meaning and allowing it to purify one's inner being. The Lord's Prayer is a credo statement containing everything necessary for sanctification. Praying it, with full awareness of its meaning, promotes spiritual growth in subtle and profound ways. The second part of this book will examine the finer nuances of the Lord's Prayer and how it can be used for both discursive and contemplative prayer.

Throughout a discursive prayer, it is helpful to intersperse moments of silence, proceeding as a cat prowls in the night, walking a few steps, then stopping to scan the environment before advancing further. Discursive prayer is two-way communication, and, likely as not, there is a message in it for you.

Contemplative Prayer

Contemplative prayer is an advanced and more refined style of prayer traditionally associated with the spiritual exercises of monastic life. It is more difficult precisely because it is easier. Its benefits are more profound yet, paradoxically, less perceptible.

While discursive and contemplative prayer share similar benefits, the final objective of each is different. Discursive prayer appeals to the intellectual centers within us. From discursive prayer we emerge with a sense of purpose, renewed meaning for our lives, an awareness of God's will in our affairs. Contemplative prayer appeals to the emotional centers within us. From contemplative prayer we emerge fortified, composed, and with a sense of wonder. We feel our oneness with God.

Instead of a stream of words, in contemplative prayer, awareness is passively concentrated on one thing: a passage of scripture, a poem, a candle, a symbol, a word or phrase silently repeated. By simply attending, we feel the fourth state of consciousness grow intense and sense God's presence without the verbal underpinnings. Indeed, the experience transcends anything we can describe.

To pray contemplatively, find a subdued environment. Assume a comfortable posture. Allow the breathing to settle. Relax the body and mind, and concentrate on a single focus, allowing everything else to fade into the background. Maintain the chosen focus for a predetermined period—five, ten, or even twenty minutes. When you notice intruding thoughts, quietly return to your focus. Doing this in one or two sessions each day makes an excellent contemplative practice.

The options for a focus for contemplative prayer are many. Liturgical phrases have been used. One of the most famous is a version of the "Jesus Prayer." It consists of an adaptation of the words of the tax collector in Luke 18:13: "Jesus Christ, Son of God, have mercy on me!"

The breathing process is an excellent medium of contemplation. One simply anchors one's awareness where the air passes in and out through the nostrils or at the base of the stomach where it expands and contracts with each breath.

Much has been written about the benefits of visualization. For example, healing is encouraged by picturing a diseased part of the body, then watching it change to an image of health. An athlete who mentally rehearses a physical performance while relaxed and fully alert will increase his or her skill. Visualizing a person or situation or condition you wish to influence will mobilize energies in that direction.

Visualizations, carefully chosen and vividly constructed, are powerful subjects for contemplative practice. One can take a passage of scripture depicting an event and recreate that event in the mind, filling in all five sensory variables: sounds, sights, smell, touch, and taste. A past experience from one's life can work equally as well, especially if one is trying to work through an unfinished or unreconciled situation.

Another popular subject for contemplation is a single, well chosen word that has a soft sound. The word *shalom* is excellent. It adds a flavor of eastern meditation while staying within the Judaic and Christian traditions. To contemplate with this word, mentally create the sound as you would any thought moving through the mind, thinking it each time you exhale. Though *shalom* means peace, it is not the meaning to which you attend but the sound. The meaning will be absorbed of its own accord.

An alternative single-word focus for contemplation is a simplified version of the Jesus prayer, or what will here be called the *Yeshua* prayer. The *Yeshua* prayer can be a powerful way of praying in that it conditions the spirit to call upon the name of Jesus, a name that can be uttered at any time.

The *Yeshua* prayer is squarely within the Christian tradition. It dates back to the apostolic age and has been practiced, in one form or another, ever since. The original form was simply to repeat the name of Jesus over and over. It has evolved to include a variety of phrases, one example being the one cited earlier, "Jesus Christ, Son of God, have mercy on me!" However, the earliest practice was simply to repeat the name of Jesus.

Yeshua, the Aramaic name for Jesus, is probably close to the original. It has an ideal sound quality and is useful both for contemplative practice and for utterances throughout the day.

One advantage of a single word like *shalom* or *Yeshua* used for contemplation is that the mind is conditioned to utter these words spontaneously at any time. One can indeed pray without ceasing; that is, one can keep a portion of awareness constantly focused in the realm of God. *Shalom* or *Yeshua*, in a contemplative exercise, is used to enter this realm. They can be employed at other times throughout the day to maintain vigilance in this realm.

For me, a most instructive image for contemplation with *shalom* or *Yeshua* is an albatross taking flight and sailing over the ocean. The stroke of its wings represent repeating the name of Jesus, *Yeshua*, or sounding the refrain, *shalom*.

On land, the albatross is an awkward bird. It must face into the wind and run along a wide stretch of beach to get airborne. Its wings are in constant motion. Once airborne, however, it sails with the air currents, beating its wings only occasionally for altitude corrections. With wings outstretched, it literally rests on the air and navigates with ease in perfect cooperation with the silent streams of air of which it uses but a small part. The albatross lives over the ocean and returns to land only to breed.

Shalom or *Yeshua* is used accordingly. In the initial stages of a contemplative exercise, the word is repeated as often as the soul struggles to transcend the material world. Once aloft in the realm of God, however, it is repeated only occasionally when one becomes aware of intruding concerns. With thoughtless freedom, one basks in the glory of God, resting on the currents of God's will. Carrying this spirit throughout the day enables one to pray without ceasing.

In addition to whatever focal subject is used for contemplation, concentrate as intently on the emptiness and silence that precedes and follows it. You are realizing solitude and silence by contrasting it with substance and sound, and it is into this silent void that you make your journey.

The focal subject of contemplation is the vehicle you ride into the realm of inner peace. During the journey, the breathing slows and even ceases for brief moments. The subject of focus sometimes spontaneously changes. *Shalom* or *Yeshua*, for example, might lengthen, shorten, or become more of an impulse than a sound. Being passive, you simply allow all this to happen.

One of the major problems of contemplation is intruding thoughts. As you repeat your word or attend to some other focus, tensions release in hidden places throughout your body, and when they do, the energy associated with these tensions is discharged, sometimes with a jerk, sometimes with a sigh, but most often by pushing a random thought through the mind.

When extraneous thoughts intrude on the contemplative process, accept them and allow them to pass. Then return to the focus of attention. Contemplation can be understood as the process of alternately focusing awareness, thinking random thoughts, and refocusing awareness. Intruding thoughts are not antagonistic to the deepening process, but part of it. As the fish works its way through the water with a side-to-side motion of its tail, this mental oscillation enables consciousness to work its way into the profound depths if the fourth state of consciousness.

Another major problem people sometimes experience with contemplation is drowsiness and a tendency to fall asleep. Over time, the novelty of a spiritual discipline wears away and the experience can become hypnotic or trance-inducing. This, of course, is counterproductive, since the nature of contemplation is not trance but relaxed alertness.

In England, during the fourteenth century, a young monk asked his teacher how to control his mind while praying. The unknown author of the Christian classic, *The Cloud of Unknowing*, wrote his response in a letter known as *The Epistle of Prayer*. Essentially, he advises his student to pray as if he might die before he finishes his prayer. There is great and subtle wisdom in this reply, for sensing the dread of nonbeing, feeling the precariousness of life, knowing the vulnerability of each moment, adds to the intensity of prayer and thus heightens concentration.

Prayer is most profound when we feel a quiet urgency. It is not the dread of a frantic urgency but the longing of a quiet urgency or expectation or need that forces us to seek God. We have but to reflect on our own experience to know that people get serious about prayer during moments of distress. How clever if we could feel the same urgency each day when we pray. Our spiritual growth would be greatly accelerated. Such quiet urgency creates hope, a yearning in our hearts for the Divine Presence to envelope our lives.

Once you have reached the depths of the fourth state of consciousness, the vehicle that has enabled the journey is left behind. It drops away of its own accord. At this point, you are standing on holy ground. In this realm of inner silence, before the Divine Presence, you are a co-creator with God. You have access not only to unbounded energy, but to unlimited creative potential. Herein lies the solution for any human dilemma, the possibilities for any human development, and the profound peace that passes all understanding.

3. The Spiritual Stance for Prayer

In the physical world, movement depends on grounding. A stance is how something makes contact with its ground. A sprinter places his feet against the starting blocks and waits for the sound of the gun. He pushes backward, against the ground, to spring forward. A building needs a foundation, a vehicle needs traction, and an athlete needs footing. Stance is crucial for the execution of any enterprise. How well something performs depends on how well it is grounded.

Metaphorically, what is true in the physical world is also true of the spiritual. To work, prayer needs grounding in a proper spiritual stance. There are three characteristics of such a stance: (1) an alert or wakeful mind, (2) the elimination of three spiritual toxins—pride, alienation, and idolatry—and (3) the ability to die unto ourselves, thus opening a center of consciousness separate from the ego that will grow into an ever complete union with God.

Wakefulness

In the Garden of Gethsemane, before leaving to pray alone, Jesus asked his disciples to stay awake and watch. After praying, he returned to find them asleep. Again he asked them to stay awake, and again, when he returned, they were asleep.

Why was it important for the disciples to remain awake? To be supportive during a time of trial? To watch for soldiers? If we examine other passages in the Bible, another explanation emerges. Both the

Old and New Testaments insist that people of God be awake and watchful, as a shepherd keeps watch over his flock at night, as a sentry stands in a watchtower and surveys the countryside. The parable of the ten maidens has as its theme remaining awake and watchful. If wakefulness is crucial for spirituality, maybe it was for their own sake that Jesus wanted his disciples to remain alert.

The significance of "wakefulness" is seen more clearly when we consider one of the biblical images of the depraved human condition, "sleep." First Thessalonians 5:6 bids us not to sleep as others do, but to stay awake. I do not believe this is an injunction to go without physical sleep. There is a spiritual sense in which people live in a trance, a slumber-like state in which the problems of today, like recurring dreams, are the recycled concerns of yesterday.

Wakefulness is a neglected theme in Christianity today. This is surprising in that wakefulness and watchfulness are virtues permeating the Bible.

Spiritual growth begins with wakefulness, a quality of consciousness that is possible only with a relaxed body, heightened awareness, and often an emotional sense of awe. A part of ourselves, a tranquil center, stands over against everything else and watches, mindful of (1) objectivity (what is other than ourselves), (2) subjectivity (our reactions within), and (3) this calm center, separate from everything else, quietly observing it all.

One winter's day, while entranced with a problem I have long since forgotten, I stood on someone's front porch and rang the door bell. Freezing rain the night before had covered everything with ice. The mid-morning sun created a spectacular, glittering world.

While waiting, I noticed a rose hip on the vine that entangled the latticed siding. It was coated with ice, neatly enclosed in a clear, crystal globe. A simple thing, quite common, but it sparkled with exquisite beauty seen nowhere else in the entire world.

That brief wait shattered all the petty concerns I was carrying. A sense of the miraculous broke through. All life was extraordinary. All events—the cracking of limbs bending with the wind, birds huddled on the chimney of the house next door, the crunch of ice beneath the tires of a passing car—seemed orchestrated as the strings of a harp plucked by the fingers of the Master's hand. And amidst it all, I felt a calm centeredness, a quality of peace that passed anything I understood.

This was a moment of wakefulness, a moment of heightened awareness. All three qualities of self-transcendence were there: a perception of otherness, a consciousness of inner reactions, and an intense awareness of my deeper self, separate from my ego.

I do not recall the problems with which I was so preoccupied. This one moment, however, is crystalline in my memory, which is one of the marks of wakefulness: the experience remains sharp in memory.

Recall, if you will, those moments in your life when you felt close to God. The one feature they all have in common is that you recall them with clarity. The more profound the experience, the more it is anchored in your memory.

Sometimes I wonder how much of the world we miss by being preoccupied with petty concerns—and concerns not so petty. Telephone calls, schedules, meetings, all have their place. However, sometimes duties and demands so consume our lives that we become blinded to the mysterious power that holds it all together. A simple walk, a look, an ear to the wind, a quiet moment now and then to connect our center with the divine, and all life takes on a new perspective.

To become conscious of our center, a part of ourselves must disconnect from everything else. It remains passive, refusing to react, and is uncritical, withholding comment on what is observed.

Unmoved, the inner observer functions even when the rest of us is distressed, quietly noticing our pettiness and judgmental attitudes, our hostilities and feelings of guilt. When we learn to identify more with this inner observer and less with day-to-day disturbances, the venom drains from our lives and we find ourselves at peace.

A hurricane is a cyclical storm with tremendous force. Always there is a calm center around which everything rotates. Gulls caught in the turbulence make their way to the eye of the storm and move with it until it blows itself out. Consciousness works in this same way. There is always a calm center around which everything rotates. We can allow our minds to become preoccupied with the wind and waves of events, identifying with the feeling of being blown about, or we can ride the wings of gulls, so to speak, to the peaceful center within.

Ridding Spiritual Toxins

Life is composed of three necessary relationships: (1) our relationship with ourselves, (2) our relationship with others, and (3) our relationship with Providence. These are necessary in the sense that they are given. They are woven into the fabric of reality. We must live with ourselves, regardless of whether or not we like ourselves. We must interact with others, regardless of whether it is smooth or trying. And we must assume a relationship to what happens to us, whether passive or reactive, optimistic or pessimistic, confident or worried.

Sin is a distortion in one or more of these relationships, a condition that creates toxins (pride, alienation, idolatry) that pollute our spiritual lives and find expressions in the nuances of our behavior. No person or group is exempt. All forms of manifest sin evolve from an individual's or group's peculiar mixture of these three poisons. It is our unique combination of these toxins that sabotages our prayer life.

Pride, or inordinate egocentrism, is a distortion of our relationship to ourselves. It emerges in consciousness as exaggerated self-importance and manifests in behavior as a persistent effort to play god. It cons us into believing we can manage life with our own resources while erasing the sense that we ultimately depend on God to create and sustain our lives. This is the greatest obstacle to prayer.

Humility is the antidote for pride. Jesus told the story of two men who went up to pray (Luke 18:9–14). The Pharisee spoke to God with pride, thanking God for his righteousness, while the tax collector prayed with humility, acknowledging his weakness. It was the tax collector, rather than the Pharisee, who was justified before God. This parable suggests that humility is a fundamental prerequisite for prayer.

Humility is not defacing oneself or pretending to be lowly. While pride is a distorted or inordinate assessment of ourselves, humility is a realistic or accurate perspective on ourselves. This includes recognizing our strong points. It also means, however, admitting our resources are not enough to sustain our lives and bring us true happiness. Humility is the willingness to look beyond ourselves to God as the source of our lives. It is this subtle surrendering that makes prayer possible; without it, prayer simply will not work.

Prayer moves awareness from its center in the ego to the center of the soul where serenity abounds and our spirits are calm. We find rest and repose in this inner sea of tranquillity and—once our familiarity with this space matures—we are able to stay centered (not off balance) and calm (not agitated), no matter what the storms of life. From this center spontaneously emerge all the answers we seek and the solution to whatever dilemma we face. Being thus centered is the essence of humility.

Alienation, or—to use the apostle Paul's term—estrangement, is a distortion of our relationship with others. Alienation evolves out of pride, for when we are puffed up with ourselves, we become estranged from others. The ever-widening gap between self and others is filled with a raging torrent of feelings such as resentment and anger, guilt and self-pity, envy and jealousy, and loneliness even in crowds. These emotional currents can stir painful memories and check our ability to pray.

The antidote for alienation is love. While alienation means feeling disconnected from others, love is recognizing our affinity, our interrelatedness with others. Love is not just a feeling. It is a recognition of a real state of affairs. Reality is structured in such a way that not only do our lives intermix through events in the manifest world, but the consciousness of each of us dips into the collective ocean of the universal Mind. We are each a wave on the same body of water. In a spiritual sense, each of us is quite literally a brother or sister to all others.

In the Sermon on the Mount, Jesus taught that if we offering a gift at the altar and remember that our brother or sister has something against us, we must first go and be reconciled. Only then do we return to the altar (Matthew 5:23–24). Whether we do this in spirit or in actuality, the passage suggests a prerequisite for prayer. In addition to humility, harmonious relationships with the people around us are crucial.

Regular prayer stabilizes our relationships by granting as broader, more encompassing perspective. It is like the difference between a quail seeing only the hedgerow and believing it sees all there is, and an eagle able to see the whole countryside. Normally, people view the world like the quail, bound to a limited perspective. Prayer grants us the eyes of an eagle, enabling us to see larger patterns in the whole network of events.

The relation between love and having a larger perspective is seen in the story of Joseph, who was greatly abused by his brothers. They beat him and threw him into a pit. Because of them, he suffered the humiliation of slavery and the accusations of Potiphar's wife. Because of them, he endured long years in prison.

When his brothers came to Egypt seeking relief from famine, Joseph had the opportunity to take revenge. Yet he forgave them. What is significant is his reasoning. "You meant this for evil," he said in effect, "but God had a bigger plan. Because of what happened years ago, many lives are now saved" (cf. Gen. 45:4–8).

If we, like Joseph, can comprehend the divine pattern in what happens, sensing the interdependence of all events, we too can forgive and thus heal our broken relationships with others. Our prayers are enhanced when we develop this larger perspective.

Idolatry, or attachment to finite ends for the sake of security, is a distortion of our relationship with God. Swept aimlessly along by the currents of life, we look for an anchor, a rock to which we can cling and which will promise security amid shifting circumstances. That to which we cling—be it family, fame, or fortune—is our idol.

In Genesis 11, the people of Babel were afraid of being scattered over the face of the earth. To ease their insecurity, they sought to build a tower with its top in the heavens. However, their language was confused, and the thing they feared was the very thing that happened. They were scattered over the face of the earth.

This scattered feeling—the dread that something might shake the foundations of our security, the fear that things will never be quite complete, the sense that something is about to go wrong—permeates all life. People are insecure and, like the people of Babel, they build towers—wealth, extensive education, success, popularity—to establish some sense of security.

As with any idolatrous enterprise, tremors always come. Since all things are finite, all things will change, all good times will end, all gods will crumble. Nothing lasts. Hence, our dreams are never complete. Our languages are always confused. We end up scattered anyway, swept away as by a mighty river.

The currents have been there all along. Only when we begin to lose our grip on security do we notice that we are clinging to a rock to try to salvage something, or swimming against the current just to stay even, or trying to push the river because things aren't moving fast enough.

All idolatrous attachments compromise prayer by lessening the need for it. Hence, most people turn to prayer only during times of crisis when their attachments are threatened.

In such moments as these, we have the opportunity to discover the antidote for idolatry, namely, faith. Faith is letting go, surrendering to the currents of God's will, flowing with events—free of fear and, all the while, knowing that God's grace will bear us up.

Three toxins—pride, alienation, idolatry—pollute our spiritual life and weaken our stance for prayer. Their antidotes—humility, love, and faith—nullify these toxins and enable the kind of stability that makes prayer possible.

These antidotes or prerequisites for prayer, when perfected, are also prayer's results. They embody the essence of sanctification, the ideal relationship to ourselves, to other people, and to God. They mature to form (1) an incredible inner peace, (2) a fluid harmony with others, and (3) an unrelenting faith, no matter how precarious circumstances may become.

Dying unto Oneself

The ego cannot tolerate humility. It wants to assert itself. Neither can it tolerate forgiveness, for it wants justice and fair play. Faith is also impossible for the ego, since it is the ego's nature to secure its own existence.

Humility, forgiving love, and faith require dying to oneself, that is, letting the ego-center die so the God-center can live. These two centers cannot coexist. People cannot serve God and Mammon. To live, we must die.

The ego, which blocks our communion with God, is actually countless ego states, hundreds of little "I ams" that show up as "me this" and "me that." Each "I am" state has its unique ideas, emotions, and mannerisms. Sometimes I am intellectual, sharing ideas. Sometimes I am angry, protesting an offense. Sometimes I am competitive, out to win.

It's like the circus act in which a clown spins a plate on top of a stick. He places the stick on a table and moves along, spinning other plates on other sticks. Before he reaches the end of the table, the first plate slows and wobbles, but he reaches it in time to give it added momentum. Eventually, the clown is frantically running up and down the length of the table to keep each plate spinning.

We laugh at the clown without realizing we are laughing at ourselves, for this is exactly how it is with our numerous ego states. We live in many worlds—our vocation, family, children, friends, projects, clubs, political causes, sports—and we are different persons in each world. Our consciousness runs frantically between worlds to keep things going. We end up feeling fractured, at loose ends, all strung out.

If we are to commune with God, each of our ego states must die. This is the most elusive of all the teachings of Jesus. We die to live. We lose our life to save it. We become servants in order to be great. We die unto ourselves so we can be "born again" and thereby enter God's kingdom. Each ego knows only its own world and is blind not only to other selves but to the Divine Presence within. Indeed, to be spiritually alive means to die. But to die and be reborn is the single most difficult thing we can ever do.

To die unto oneself means to disconnect ourselves from the countless "I am" states that consume our lives. It means taking our many selves less seriously. It means being in the world but not of the world (cf. John 17:15, 16).

In a way, this is like splitting in two, allowing our hidden observer to transcend or rise above our ego states. Such self-transcendence as a stance for prayer is a special inner separation, not one ego state divided against another but a separation between our real self and our numerous little selves. It's becoming a silent watcher in the center of the kaleidoscope of events that make up our lives.

The Divine Intelligence that orchestrates reality dwells within each person. It is an eternal "I am" presence, the image of God that dwells in each of us. It is our real self, buried far below the egos of which we are normally aware. This pearl of great price and the aura of peace that surrounds it is literally the kingdom of God within us. To make contact with the divine center, to become one with it, is the sum of everything religion is about and the goal of all praying.

Part II: Praying the Lord's Prayer

4. The Inner Structure of the Lord's Prayer

For a contemplative exercise, begin by reading Matthew 22:36–40. It may be helpful to use this text each day for a week and, on the various days of the week, to read from different versions. This passage suggests the twofold structure of scriptural truth (our relationship with God and our relationship to the world) found throughout the Bible and particularly in the Lord's Prayer.

Next, go through the five preparatory steps for prayer as outlined in chapter two. Attune yourself to the environment of your private sanctuary. Adjust your posture. Allow your breathing to settle. Physically and mentally relax. For fifteen or twenty minutes, concentrate on this passage from Matthew.

You may wish to imagine the events of this passage in detail. See the crowds gathered about Jesus. Note their clothing, the covered faces of the women watching from the sides and the wrinkled faces of the men staring at Jesus. Smell the dry air, the scent of produce from a nearby marketplace, or the stench of sweat from camels under heavy loads. Hear the commotion in the background, the sounds of people trading, and the bleating of a goat tied to a stake. Notice the Pharisees huddled together in the distance, and one of them leading the others to Jesus. Watch his gesture, the lifting of his hand as he proceeds to ask a question. Hear the quality of his voice. Listen to his question. Allow the scene to unfold as Jesus pauses, then answers. Internally experience this scene with all your senses.

You may prefer a less active exercise, such as repeating over and over to yourself the two phrases in Jesus' answer: *Love the Lord your God with all your heart, mind, soul, and strength*, and *love your neighbor as yourself*. Hear the words as if coming from somewhere other than yourself and addressing you. Imagine that you hear the voice of Jesus, or perhaps the voice of God, speaking to you personally.

The purpose of this exercise is to build a foundation for experiencing the Lord's Prayer by grasping its inner structure. The more solid the foundation, the more penetrating the prayer.

In learning the Lord's Prayer, the destination (mastering the prayer) is not as important as the journey (doing the exercises). In seminary, while walking down a hallway, I overheard a professor's observation to a group of students. I almost missed his comment when I walked past. He said, "Sometimes it may take you all afternoon to read just one page of scripture." Like most students, I had a compulsion to get through the material. Speed reading was in vogue. It hadn't occurred to me that reading the Bible slowly, and with frequent pauses for reflection might be better.

There is a basic truth in this professor's comment that is relevant to all aspects of life. A person out for an afternoon stroll will see things a jogger will miss. The same is true for the Lord's Prayer. Speed through the material and not only will you miss the scent of flowers along the way, but the end result will be less than what it could be. Go slow and do each exercise; eventually, your spiritual growth will be substantial.

What follows is information to augment the above contemplative exercise. By itself, the information is not as significant as what you will gain from the experience of the exercise.

Two Realms of Experience: Outer and Inner

Consciousness can focus on two realms. On the one hand, we are aware of the outer world through our senses. We see green grass and blue skies. We hear birds singing and the breeze playing in the branches.

On the other hand, we are aware of our inner world, which is seemingly accessible only to each of us individually. This world is filled with sensations, emotions, thoughts, images, and impulses.

In the outer world, we can extend our senses with microscopes, telescopes, amplifiers, and a host of other devices. We can also project ourselves into the outer world by extending our hands and feet with tools and various modes of transportation. Technology amplifies and extends sensory-motor capacities to enable a great range of abilities.

Likewise, we can extend our inner world through such things as prayer, meditation, symbolic and sacramental imagery, parables, and devotional material. By doing this, we enter a singular realm, a holistic and spiritual dimension that transcends the distinction between inner and outer. This realm is filled with inner peace and unified by an all-embracing Divine Presence.

This twofold structure of experience has often led to a dualism between the sacred and the profane. Many religions assume such a dualism, explicitly or implicitly, suggesting that the material is somehow opposed to the spiritual. Such ascetic attitudes, in one way or another, encourage people to deny the secular world in order to grow spiritually.

But the sacred and the spiritual are intertwined. Each realm of consciousness affects the other. People are happiest when they live in harmony with both God and manifest reality. This is recognized throughout the Bible.

The three necessary relationships mentioned in the third chapter—our relationship with ourselves, with others, and with God—play out in two arenas: the inner world and the outer world. The vertical, inner dimension, is where we wrestle with our relationship to God. The horizontal, outer dimension is where we interact with others and the world in which we live.

The story of Adam and Eve exemplifies the drama and the problems in the first arena. Their fundamental temptation was to play god, knowing good and evil. Today, people try to play god in their private worlds, struggling to manage their lives by themselves and forcing their own standards of right and wrong on others. The vertical brokenness—the separation between ourselves and God—has its counterpart in a horizontal brokenness as exemplified in the story of Cain and Abel. Just as Cain's countenance fell, causing him to strike out against his brother, all people become alienated (in one way or another) from others and from the world in which they live. This twofold brokenness and the interplay between them underlies all the "soap opera" dramas that constitute human existence.

Throughout the Bible, God's word is structured to address this twofold separation. Indeed, the biblical message can be understood as God's effort to heal this twofold brokenness. Just as the two stories of the Fall (Adam and Eve, Cain and Abel) are structured to explain our twofold problem, so the Ten Commandments are designed to offer the Old Testament's twin solution to the problem. The first four commandments deal with our relationship to God: have no other gods before the one God; honor the Sabbath and keep it holy; don't take the Lord's name in vain; make no graven images. The last six commandments deal with our relationship to others: you shall not steal, kill, bear false witness, etc. The commonly used symbol of the Ten Commandments—two tablets, side-by-side—reflects this division: four Roman numerals on the left, six on the right.

When Jesus summarized the law, he kept this dual structure (Matthew 22:36-40). The most important commandment he gave first. We are to love God with our heart, mind, soul, and strength. The second commandment he compared with the first. We are to love our neighbors as ourselves. What makes these two commandments fundamental is his following comment: "On these two commandments depend all the law and the prophets." These two commandments summarize the essence of religion.

In both the Ten Commandments and Jesus' summary of the law, the vertical precedes the horizontal. Our relationship with God is primary and forms the foundation upon which we relate to others. The writer of 1 John recognizes the extent to which this twofold relationship is glued together:

> But if we live our lives in the light,
> as he is in the light,
> we are in union with one another, . . .
> let us love one another
> since love comes from God
> and everyone who loves is begotten by God and knows God.
> Anyone who fails to love can never have known God,
> because God is love (1 John 1:7; 4:7-8 JB).

Once our relationship with God is healthy, our relationship with others also becomes healthy.

This twofold structure of experience—an inner and an outer, and the brokenness possible in each—forms the basis of the Lord's Prayer. The first three petitions address our relationship with God. The last three address our relationship to the world in which we live.

The First Three Petitions

Spiritual health requires that we first receive the healing of our estrangement from God. The first three petitions of the Lord's Prayer provide the means for this by forming an interrelated sequence of affirmations through which we (1) become aware of the basic nature of God, (2) sense this basic nature within us, and (3) seek to align our intentions with it.

The first petition deals with God's glory, *Hallowed be thy name.* This not only consecrates or affirms the sacredness of God's name, but it also recognizes the essential nature of God. (In scripture, "name" signifies the essential nature of the thing or person named.) When we pray this petition, we recognize God's creative power as the basis of all reality.

The second petition deals with God's presence, *Thy kingdom come.* This initiates our awareness of God's peace within. Here, God's essential nature, recognized in the first petition, is allowed to reign within us (or, when prayed by a group, among us).

The third petition deals with God's intentions, *Thy will be done.* This surrenders our personal will to the course of the Divine. This petition seeks to move the recognition of the first petition and the inner peace of the second petition into the practical aspects of life.

Coming full circle—realizing God's presence, sensing it within, bringing it out—heals our separation from God.

Most commentaries append the transitions statement, *on earth as it is in heaven,* to the third petition. Actually, it can follow any of the first three petitions and, hence, can be thought of as applying to all three. This transition statement is an affirmation of the twofold structure of the Lord's Prayer. By affirming the manifestations of the Divine (in heaven) as realities within the world in which we live (on earth), this statement distinguishes the vertical from the horizontal and sets the stage for the final three petitions.

The Last Three Petitions

Once our separation from God is healed, we address our insecurities in the world. The last three petitions embrace our entire temporal experience: the present (daily bread), the past (transgressions), and the future (temptations). When prayed with full comprehension, this prayer enables us to heal our alienations and soothe our insecurities in the world.

The fourth petition, *Give us this day our daily bread,* secures the whole reality of the present by asking for daily bread, the symbol for everything we need to sustain our lives for just one day. Life is precarious; there are no guarantees. When praying this petition, we build our trust that God will sustain us.

The fifth petition, *Forgive us our debts as we forgive our debtors*, heals the past with forgiveness. We erase our guilt by claiming total absolution, and we free ourselves of resentment by forgiving everyone who has ever offended us.

The final petition, *Leave us not in our trials but deliver us from evil*, acknowledges that the world is a maze laced with pitfalls and asks God to guide us through it. (The reasons for translating this petition as we do here will be given in chapter sixteen.) In this petition, in addition to asking for guidance, we particularly seek deliverance from the wrong to which we can easily fall prey.

Often, when people say the Lord's Prayer, they gloss over it, little realizing it speaks to the entire realm of experience, both vertical and horizontal, both inward and outward. Anyone who prays this prayer regularly and with ever-deepening awareness of what it means is on the road to spiritual perfection, both in the kingdom of God and in the kingdoms of this world. Such a person will eventually receive inner peace and be a positive influence for harmony in the world in which he or she lives.

5. The Imperative Tone of the Lord's Prayer

As a contemplative exercise, begin by reading Matthew 7:7-11. In this formula for prayer, notice the tone of insistence. *Ask*, and you *will* receive. *Seek*, and you *will* find. *Knock*, and it *will* be opened to you. There is a quality of spiritual assertiveness in these verses.

After reading this passage, follow the five steps for contemplation outlined in chapter two, repeating the words *ask and you will receive, seek and you will find, knock and it will be opened to you.* You may wish to use three breaths for each cycle, one for each phrase. Pronounce each phrase to yourself as you exhale. This exercise will refine your ability to concentrate and develop your confidence in prayer.

An alternative focus for this contemplative exercise is the word *shalom*, which means peace in a holistic sense. *Shalom* implies everything necessary for total peace, both inner peace and peace within the surrounding community. (Using this word for contemplation was discussed in chapter two.) While pronouncing *shalom*, feel the insistence. Say it as if you are calling into being the many things *shalom* implies.

To remind yourself of the twofold division discussed in the last chapter, you may wish to use a third alternative, using as a focus of concentration two phrases, *inner peace* and *outer harmony*, each repeated separately when breathing out. Again, feel the insistence. This will instill in the mind the qualities you hope for as a result of prayer.

Whatever focus you choose for this exercise, it is critical to employ an imperative mood. Instead of experiencing the words as coming from somewhere else, as in the last exercise, experience them as coming from you. Insist. You are not practicing positive thinking here, inducing your own self-confidence and producing your own good fortune. You are opening yourself to God's address of your life. What you want to learn is to do it intentionally.

As a child of God, you are the heir of the blessings divinely promised and you are, in effect, demanding your rights. Sensing the mood of insistence will instill the proper frame of mind for saying the Lord's Prayer.

The Need to Insist

Several years ago while serving as pastor of an inner city church, I officiated at a wedding for a black couple, a large wedding with five groomsmen and five bridesmaids. The wedding proceeded smoothly, in spite of a minor conflict at the rehearsal. There was something about being white that gave me a problem of authority with the black groomsmen. When I asked them to line up, they ignored me and made snide comments to each other.

I expressed my frustration to the mother of the bride. This large, heavy-set woman doubled up her fists, marched to the front and shouted, "You boys get yourselves over here, right now!" That was the quickest, straightest line of young men you ever saw.

She had spoken with an imperative tone. What I had used was a mild-mannered, easygoing, indicative tone. The indicative mood conveys facts or makes requests, while the imperative insists or makes demands.

In English there is no way to indicate the mood in the verb by its spelling. We show the mood by the way we arrange words or punctuate sentences. In the above anecdote, I indicated the imperative mood by the exclamation mark at the end of the sentence.

The Greek language, the language of the New Testament, indicates the mood of the verb by its spelling. The verbs in the Lord's Prayer, being in the imperative mood, suggest an unusual insight. When first considered, this may seem rash. It's like waging a protest before God, presenting a list of demands. "Here they are! This is what we expect! *Give* us this day our daily bread! *Forgive* us our debts." It violates our sense of good manners, for we are taught to say "please" when asking for something. It feels rude to insist. When we think of praying, we think of politely asking God for things.

The imperative tone of the Lord's Prayer is a lesson in expectation. Because we expect service from God, we get it. Indeed, any prayer works better with spiritual assertiveness, for it is precisely the insisting that calls forth our foreordained blessings. And the more intense the insistence, the more likely the blessings.

The incredible secret is this: God has already given us these things. All blessings swim in an ocean of unrealized potentials, living as divine ideas in a vast spiritual realm. As surely as an acorn contains within it the complete idea of the oak, when an endeavor begins, it embraces all possible conclusions. A baby crawls on the living room floor enveloped in all potentialities for its entire life. Prayer is reaching into the great sea of possibilities and claiming what is already ours. By God's grace it is given.

Indeed, this is the essence of the creative process. Anything created is first conceived. Before a building is constructed, it is envisioned; then the blueprints are drawn. Before a career is realized, a person dreams of what he might be, then strives to realize what is hoped for. Conception precedes manifestation, and it is this truth that enables prayer.

Expectancy is the energy of faith. The value of an expectant attitude and its relationship with faith is found throughout the Bible. When Moses led the people of Israel to the southern edge of the Promised Land, he sent out twelve spies. They returned with conflicting reports. Two spies, Joshua and Caleb, expected victory based on a faith in God's promise. Ten spies were frightened, saying in effect, "The men were so big we felt like grasshoppers standing next to them. We can't possible take the land." Their fears spread throughout the crowd. Because the people of Israel envisioned defeat, Moses knew it would be futile to wage an attack. They wandered in the wilderness forty years before a more "foolish" generation, one wise enough to be courageous, came along. Only then did the Israelites insist on claiming God's promise. The expectant attitude was the prerequisite for victory.

Much later, Gideon called together an army, only to discover the Israelites were outnumbered by the Midianites. Still, Gideon sent home those who were frightened and did not believe in victory. From those remaining, he chose only those who were alert. (Soldiers who lifted water to their mouths maintained eye contact with their surroundings. Those who put their faces in the water compromised their awareness.) Gideon and his three hundred men won the battle because of a reckless abandon born of a silent faith in God's providential possibilities.

Thoughout the Lord's Prayer, God's realities are already given. It is the expectant attitude that brings them into consciousness. God's name is already hallowed in that God's essence, by its very nature, is sacred. God's kingdom is already a present reality. Only our blindness hides it from us. Our daily bread is already given to us in the realm of what is possible, awaiting only our recognition of it. The word "forgiveness" breaks down as "fore-given." It is something given to us before we need it. The imperative mood of the verb calls what already exists into consciousness and thereby encourages its manifestation in reality.

Children have no troubles insisting on what they want. A baby protests when hungry, the message being, "Feed me right now! Give me this instant my daily bread!" The baby assumes the world is there to take care of it. So it insists. When we pray the Lord's Prayer, God, like a loving parent, responds with all the patience and love necessary for the moment.

In the Sermon on the Mount, Jesus said, "Ask, and it will be given you; seek, and you will find; knock, and it will be opened to you. For every one who asks receives, and he who seeks finds, and to him who knocks it will be opened" (Matt. 7:7–8). Notice the insistence, the imperative mood. Believe it, expect it, insist upon it; and, at some deep level, it becomes so. This is the imperative mood of the Lord's Prayer.

6. The Corporate Nature of the Lord's Prayer

One way to incorporate the Lord's Prayer into consciousness is to use each phrase as a focus for concentration in a contemplative exercise. This will be the plan for this and subsequent chapters. For the next contemplative exercise, use the phrase *Our Father*. Enter into your prayer chapel, assume a comfortable posture, and allow your breathing to settle. Relax your body and mind. Then, for fifteen to twenty minutes, think the phrase *Our Father* each time to exhale.

Referring to God as "Father" as opposed to "Mother" probably originated and is certainly sustained by culturally bound traditions. Since the relationship with God as defined in the Lord's Prayer is so intensely personal, gender may affect your ability to identify with God. It would be a mistake to allow traditional usage to rob you of your access to the Lord's Prayer. The truth in the parental metaphor refers to God's creative and sustaining power: He/She is the source of our being and the one who provides our living. What matters is that the metaphor convey this truth. For some, using *Mother* can be more meaningful. Whatever the choice of words, remember that gender as well as the parental image itself is secondary to the truth to which they point. It is only due to the limitations of language that the image of "fatherhood" permeates this discussion.

As you sink into contemplative experience, savor the sound and feel the significance of each word, especially the word *our*. Become aware of the providential care of God for all people, all communities of people, and particularly the various communities with which you are associated.

Recognizing the sovereignty of God over all creation is more than a cognitive exercise. All people and events are inextricably tied together. Our salvation and the blessings we enjoy are worked out in and through community. Being aware of the creative and sustaining power of God over all things and events expands our consciousness to include the larger networks of which each of us is a part.

An Instructive Story

After Moses made his final departure into the wilderness, Joshua assumed leadership of the Israelites. He led them across the Jordan River, where they faced the first obstacle in laying claim to the Promised Land—the walled city of Jericho.

What happened next is one of the most brilliant examples of human courage and military strategy found anywhere. In dead silence, once each day for six days, the Israelites marched around Jericho. On the seventh day, they circled the city seven times, again in silence. After the seventh time around, they stopped and stared.

Imagine how tense people must have been inside the walls of Jericho, day after day, watching this strange clan of nomads encircle their city, not knowing what to expect nor when they might strike. It would have been sheer terror.

All of a sudden, without warning, the Israelites shouted, blew their trumpets, and broke jars. The walls crumbled and fell, the city was destroyed, and not one Israelite was lost in the process.

There are several lessons to be learned from Joshua: for example, the intricate blend of divine possibilities and human cunning and the importance of expectancy in achieving God's will. Another truth, one as profound as it is subtle, emerges as the story unfolds.

In keeping with the Israelite practice of giving first fruits to God, Joshua celebrated the victory over Jericho by placing a ban on the city. There was to be no looting. Achan surveyed the ruins. Gold and silver on the ground. Tent poles and cooking utensils scattered about. All of it seemed too good to be wasted. Achan couldn't resist. He took some of the treasures for himself and hid them in his tent.

When the Israelites entered their battle against the city of Ai, they were defeated. Confused, Joshua prayed and discovered Achan's treachery. He ordered the execution of Achan and his family and had all the goods of Achan's household destroyed. When the Israelites again went into battle, they won.

Beyond Individualism

By our contemporary standards, this seems a strange tale. Because one man broke the ban, the whole community suffered defeat. Why would God hold the nation accountable for the crimes of one citizen? And why punish wives and children for the crimes of the father? It doesn't seem fair. It's like sentencing a man to the gas chamber and sending his family with him.

American individualism—with its concern for individual rights and reverence for personal merit—characterized the frontier spirit. It made our nation strong by encouraging the survival of the fittest in a land not yet tame. Rugged individualism is bred into our thinking. Children learn to compete for grades and trophies. Books that teach people how to get rich, stay ahead, and look out for number one flood the market. In such a culture, community life can be understood, but corporate responsibility (not voluntary, but based on the very structure of reality) boggles the mind. We believe that people stand before the law as individuals, guilty or innocent.

The Israelites, by contrast, lived under a concept of justice foreign to our modes of thought. This makes the story of Joshua difficult to understand. Family units and whole communities were held to be guilty or innocent because of the acts of one person.

There is a sense in which the Israelite pattern of justice represents the structure of reality. Each of us is a literal extension of everyone else. Our lives are intricately woven together. I cannot sit in a restaurant and order a cup of coffee without participating in the lives of countless people, everyone from the waitress who serves me to the Peruvian hands that picked the coffee beans.

This built-in interconnectedness of experience implies a corporate responsibility. A community is accountable for the actions of each citizen; and the effects of each person's behavior, whether for good or ill, ripples throughout the whole society. When one individual does well, it strengthens the whole. On the other hand, just as the strength of a chain is measured by its weakest link, should one individual fall short, the whole is diminished.

As a youth, I played a trumpet in the high school band. One clarinet player was notorious for her lack of practice. I remember a concert in which the music built to the most intense moment, then paused before the finale. During that precious and sacred moment—*squeak*. After the concert, everyone filed back to the band room like

Israelite soldiers returning from their first engagement with the city of Ai, dragging swords and carrying wounded bodies. I remember how unjust it seemed. No matter how much the rest of us had practiced, what was noticed was that one, isolated, irritating squeak.

When one person errs, the consequences are borne by the entire group. This fact is not a matter of choice. It is built into the natural order of things.

Corporate accountability, when violated, results in "corporate guilt," a concept foreign to modern jurisprudence (with the possible exception of the Nuremburg trials). It is not "guilt" in a psychological sense; that is, it is not a feeling. Nor is it a guilt in the modern legal sense, as when describing an individual's status when in violation of a law. Corporate responsibility and corporate guilt refer to a condition that exists naturally in the complex web of human interaction. When Joshua executed Achan and his family, it was like cutting a cancer out of a body. Maybe a few healthy cells were destroyed in the process, but the integrity of the whole was considered more important than the individual parts. The operation, though painful, was thought necessary.

Corporate responsibility is fundamental in biblical thought, not only in the Old Testament as in the story of Achan, but in the New Testament as well. The early church was a community in which property was held in common. Imagine the trust necessary for a whole church to share the same checking account and for each member to receive an equal allowance. In the fifth chapter of Acts, Ananias and Sapphira sold their property and gave it to the communal store, but they cheated by keeping a portion of the profit. Peter confronted them with such intensity that each, in turn, died. As with Joshua, the purity of the community depended on purging its ranks of corruption. In the climate of first century persecution, integrity among Christians was essential. The group's survival depended on it.

The Lord's Prayer Is Corporate

The Lord's Prayer presupposes community. Nine times throughout the prayer a reference is made to community: *Our* Father in heaven; give *us our* daily bread; forgive *us our* debts as *we* have forgiven *our* debtors; leave *us* not in temptation, but deliver *us* from evil. It is not just personal concerns we espouse, but those of the various communities in which we live. When we pray the Lord's Prayer, saying *Our Father*, we capture a sense of corporate responsibility (the awareness of our complex interconnectedness with others) and bring it under the sovereignty of God.

Corporate responsibility, regardless of whether we sense it or accept personal responsibility for it, is a fundamental force in our lives. Whatever the system, each member supports the whole, and the whole is responsible for each member. Praying *our* in the Lord's Prayer enables us to assume our place within the communities of which we are a part. It's like geese flying south in the familiar V formation. Researchers believe the lead goose does the work by cutting through the air. Each goose on each side of the V rides the wake of the one in front of it. When the lead goose grows tired, it drops to the end of the line, allowing the next goose to assume the lead. Geese flying in formation can travel as much as forty percent farther than if each goose winged its way alone. Prayer is most effective when we find our place in the corporate network of relationships in which we live.

7. The Personal Relationship of the Lord's Prayer

The spiritual exercise associated with this chapter is the same as the last with one exception. As a focus for concentration, instead of the phrase *Our Father*, use the phrase *My Father*. Not only is there biblical precedent for using the first person, this exercise anchors in consciousness the intense personal relationship each of us has with God.

God Is Our *Abba*

Jesus used "*Abba*, the Aramaic word for father, to refer to God. The only time he referred to God in other terms was on the cross, when he cried out, "My God. my God, why hast thou forsaken me?" (Matt. 27:46).

People in the first century referred to God as father but did not use the word *Abba*. Other than what is attributed to Jesus, nowhere in early documents is there an example of such usage. This reference, unique with Jesus, was so unusual that New Testament writers made note of it in Mark 14:36, Romans 8:15, and Galatians 4:6.

Abba was an Aramaic word used by children. Today, parents gather about the cribs of their infants to make faces and mutter baby-talk, encouraging their children to say ma-ma or da-da. Should a child say the magic word, parents cheer, and the baby, with eyes wide, squeals, knowing something right was said. Parents of the first century were no different. When Aramaic fathers leaned over the crib, the word they used for da-da was *abba*.

Jesus chose this expression to refer to the divine-human relationship. It carried all the feelings of closeness implied in the English expression "Daddy." By using this image and teaching it to others, Jesus apparently wanted to establish a new way of relating to God. So special was this relationship that he said, on one occasion, "Call no man your 'Abba' (Father)" (Matt. 23:9). For the disciples, this concept and the feelings associated with it were reserved solely for God.

In the last chapter, we examined the corporate nature of the Lord's Prayer, the fact that the pronouns in the prayer imply community. This is probably due to the early church's liturgical use of the prayer. Without minimizing the truth embedded in the plural pronouns, it may be recognized that Jesus addressed God primarily as "*My* Abba"; and when he spoke to others, he referred to God as "*Your* Abba."

These personal references, coupled with the connotations of the Aramaic "Abba," carry profound implications regarding our relationship with God. The use of "my" and "your" and "Abba" defines our relationship with God as that of an offspring to a parent. It carries all the innocence and intimacy, trust and dependency, privacy and simplicity implied in such a relationship.

When we say the Lord's Prayer, or any other prayer, and address God as *Father* or *Mother*, we remind ourselves of our close, personal relationship with God. The mood of this relationship constitutes the soil within which the rest of our prayers germinate. The beauty and comfort, the depth of insight, gained from prayer directly depends on the fertility of this soil.

Years ago, as a counselor in a church camp, I asked a group of young people to paraphrase the Lord's Prayer. They were to use synonyms or original phrases for the major words in the prayer. One young man began with, "Hey, Big Daddy in the Sky!" At first I was unsettled by the apparent disrespect. Then the phrase grew on me, and I now appreciate it as a good rendering. "Hey" captures the urgency of the imperative tone that follows. "Big" suggests majesty and "Daddy" embraces the personal relationship. "In the Sky"? Well, it's not perfect.

What I especially liked about this young man's rendering is its offense, its seeming irreverence. Possibly, with all the liturgical pomp of first century religion, to use a child's utterance for God was equally as offensive. However, what "Abba" sacrifices in formality, it gains in affinity or closeness.

Our Closeness to God

A mother and father take their daughter to a shopping center and meander through the crowds. Taking two steps to their one, and not particularly interested in anything outside the toy store, the little girl quickly grows tired. No problem. Her father carries her. Indifferent to the whole world and with tiny arms draped around his neck, she sleeps. Confident in her dependency and knowing everything is cared for, she lets the world go on. This is a perfect picture of the Abba relationship.

Any father who has ever placed his son on a kitchen counter, stepped back, and invited him to to jump, has witnessed the essence of the Abba relationship. The counter is higher than the child is tall. Still, he leaps. Even when the father steps back farther, and though there may be a moment of wide-eyed hesitation, reckless abandon soon takes over. The child knows the father will catch him.

The essence of our Abba relationship with God is in the realization of God's affinity. God is closer to us than we are to ourselves. Losing touch with God is like losing a pencil and plowing through the papers on your desk to find it. You had it a minute ago. Surely, it's here somewhere. Then you discover it behind your ear. You looked in things around you, when actually it was next to you.

The truth was beautifully illustrated for me one time when my son was small. We played a game in which he left the room and I hid an object. When he returned to search, I gave him clues by saying, "You're getting warmer," or "You're getting cooler," depending on how close or far he was from the object. What I hid was a Tinker-Toy trinket he had made. Once, as he left the room, I hooked it over the back belt loop of his blue jeans. When he returned, it was still there. Everywhere he went, I said, "You're getting warmer; you're so very close!" However, he never found it. The irony of his searching has stuck with me as a metaphor for the way people seek God, constantly probing outward for something that hides deep within.

Once, when in a hurry to leave the house, I couldn't find my car keys. Frantically I searched the table and dresser, places where I thought I might have left them, only to discover I had them tightly clutched in my fist. In this same way, we try many ways to find a close, personal relationship with God. We read books, listen to tapes, ponder sermons, all to better know God. However, what we seek is not out there, in the world. It is within, and only as we journey within do we discover what has been there all along.

There is a story told (the source of which escapes me) about creation. When God created the world, he assigned many of the responsibilities to committees. He gave one group of angels a most important task: find a place to hide the keys to the kingdom of heaven. "Hide them where only a few will find them," God instructed, "for the world can handle only a limited number of enlightened people."

The committee convened to consider the problem. "Hide them in the clouds," one angel suggested. "People are bound to the earth."

"That won't work," came the rebuttal. "People will one day learn to fly."

"Hide them in the ocean," someone suggested. "People are bound to the land."

"That won't work," came another rebuttal, "for the day will come when people will explore every corner of the earth."

"Then hide them in the moon."

"No," said another. "One day, people will even reach the moon."

Finally, one angel, who had been silent through much of the discussion, spoke, "Hide them in people's hearts. If people are so busy looking outside themselves, the safest place would be in the deepest recesses of their inner worlds."

Silence fell on the group. That was it. From that day to this, the keys to God's kingdom are hidden where they are least likely to be found. Only as we explore the hidden spaces within will we ever discover the keys to God's kingdom. Such exploration begins as we recognize our personal relationship with God as implied in the phrase *My Father*.

8. The Transcendent Dimension of the Lord's Prayer

Another helpful contemplative exercise is to use *who art in heaven* as a focus for concentration. While doing so, capture a sense of the otherness of God. Having grounded your consciousness in the feeling of closeness with God using the phrase *Our Father*, now remind yourself of the distance. God's perspective is not the same as the ego's.

As you are seated in your prayer chapel, relax and breathe evenly. Notice the things around you—sights, sounds, sensations. Become aware of the events that have happened in the recent past and some of the things that might soon happen. Feel all these things as somehow contained in God while at the same time removed from God.

Throughout the Bible, the otherness of God is recognized. More often than not, people experience God as absent and feel a need to wait for God's presence to be made known. While God is closer to us than we are to ourselves, there is, paradoxically, a great chasm between ourselves and God. This separation finds expression in the Lord's Prayer. Grasp the significance of the images in the Lord's Prayer that indicate this distance—on earth, in heaven. Experience the manifest world as "on earth" while sensing the Creative Force behind it all as "in heaven."

As I was directing a youth retreat, a young woman in her early teens approached me and asked me to pray for her mother.

"What's the matter with your mother?" I asked.

This youth explained how unreasonable her mother was, not allowing her to stay out past midnight and scolding her for not cleaning her room.

We talked several minutes, and she still believed that her mother had the problem. She insisted I pray for her mother so God would "fix it."

I asked her what she would do to help the relationship if I prayed for the situation.

"Nothing," she replied. "If we turn it over to God, he'll take care of it."

This young woman envisioned herself as religious, carrying a Bible and perpetually quoting scriptures. She was angered when I told her I would not pray for her in the way she wanted. After much discussion, she agreed to come back later with a few concrete ideas about what she might do to improve the situation. If she was willing to be an active participant in God's healing, we agreed, then we would talk about prayer.

This young woman's approach to prayer is typical of many people. They assume God's perspective is the same as their own and that prayer secures a divine endorsement for their own design of how things should be.

This is *spiritual confluence*, a condition in which one loses the sense of boundary between one's own ego center and the God center within. In spiritual confluence, people believe their perceptions and wishes are the expression of God's will, and they resist any suggestion to the contrary. After all, they ask, how can "God" be wrong?

It is easy to develop a spiritual confluence because we are bound to a single vantage point. Each of us comprehends the world from his or her own perspective. We can imagine how the world seems to someone else, or to God, but we cannot know for sure. It seems almost natural to assume that God sees the world exactly as we do and hears things solely through our ears.

Such confluence is the basis of fanaticism. Sometimes, nations and groups of people justify their expansion and oppression with a belief in their own "manifest destiny." They are slow to acknowledge that the destiny of others might also be manifest.

Once, while jogging along a residential street during the early hours of a summer evening, I attracted a pack of eight or ten dogs of a variety of breeds. Each was feeling the call of the wild and had joined the pack to pass the hours of the night prowling neighborhoods and chasing joggers. I was their next victim.

I couldn't outrun them, so I turned and stared into the eyes of the leader, a German shepherd who had stopped at the curb. Amidst a swelling cacophony of barking, all dogs followed suit except a basset hound who apparently didn't catch the signal of the leader. With ears flopping, it charged right up to my ankles.

I continued to defy the German shepherd but watched the basset hound from the corner of my eye. Its four stocky legs seemed short compared to its long body set low to the ground. It sniffed my shoes and then glanced at the leader, who was still poised at the curb.

Only then did it realize it had overextended itself. Slowly its once proud tail dropped between its hind legs. It lowered its head and looked up with sad eyes. Without its backers, all the bravery drained from its body. I reached down and patted the hound, then slowly backed away, careful not to excite another chase. This little dog scampered back to the security of the pack, embarrassed, I'm sure.

I strolled on for several blocks, pondering the analogies in what had happened. Sometimes, people ally with religion in the same way this basset hound joined the pack. Particularly when they feel insecure and nurse a low self-esteem, they adopt a cause greater than themselves, an alter ego which enables them to feel important or powerful or a champion of "justice" or the "right" way. Such fanatics may believe God is on the throne of their lives and that it is God's kingdom they espouse. In reality, however, their ego is in charge and they are playing God.

It's ironic that Jesus had a greater affinity for sinners and the oppressed than he did for the religious enthusiasts of his day. Tax collectors, drunkards, and prostitutes felt his compassion, while Pharisees received his rebuke.

I grew up believing the Pharisees were "bad guys," wearing black hats and hiding in caves. The Pharisees were exponents of the law, models of righteousness, teachers of religion. Jesus' rebuke suggests there is something very precarious about being religious and engaging in a life of prayer.

As was discussed in the last chapter, when prayer begins we remind ourselves of our closeness with God. God is closer to us than we are to ourselves. The salutation of the Lord's Prayer, *Our Father*, recognizes this closeness, thus neutralizing feelings of abandonment within the turbulence of day-to-day events. Prayer, however, needs a safety valve, a mechanism to balance the egocentric pressures that build up when we approach God and feel our intense closeness with the Divine Presence.

Immediately after we affirm God's closeness, we remind ourselves of the distance by saying *who art in heaven*. This does not mean that

God is remote. It means the realm of Deity is "deeper" or "other than" our egos, our thoughts, our feelings, our desires. Saying this phrase is the mechanism that keeps our perspective in balance and helps us avoid the perils of spiritual confluence.

A person is either ego-centered or God-centered. The difference is deceptively subtle, so much so that one may think he or she is God-centered and still favor egocentric concerns.

By instilling within consciousness the radical otherness of God, we keep our sense of closeness with God from becoming distorted by an egocentric identification.

When we add the phrase *who art in heaven* to our prayers, we establish the delicate but necessary balance between the two realms within which we live, the material and the spiritual. This balance must be maintained if Christians are to advance their spiritual journeys.

While praying *Our Father* prepares the soil from which the rest of our prayers spring, adding *who art in heaven* provides the light toward which they grow. This growth is always beyond the self and toward the Source that transcends the ego. Without this phrase, prayer becomes like sprouts in an amber jar. Because they lack room, roots and stalks tangle about each other. Because they lack light, they remain pale.

The phrase *who art in heaven* is the antidote built into the Lord's Prayer to neutralize pride. It averts the spiritual confluence or the tendency to identify God with one's ego that results in fanaticism. Praying *who art in heaven* keeps us from thinking of God as a divine satellite orbiting around our own self-interests.

9. The Hallowing of God's Name

When done regularly, physical exercise tones the body. In the same way, when persistently and conscientiously done, spiritual exercises attune the soul to God. As in physical exercise, regularity is a key. For a contemplative exercise that will deepen your understanding of the nature and sanctity of God, use as a focus for concentration the phrase *hallowed be thy name*.

Unlike the final three petitions of the Lord's Prayer, in which the verbs (give, forgive, leave, deliver) are active, the verbs of the first three petitions (be, come, be) are passive. You are not invoking something, such as daily bread or forgiveness, but rather affirming a condition of being and, in doing so, bringing into consciousness what already is real.

During this contemplative exercise, you are seeking a special way of knowing, one which engages the heart as well as the head. Sink into the experience. Develop an understanding of the nature of God that you are declaring sacred while feeling, at a deep level, the intensity of this sacredness.

If someone reads a book on exercise but fails to go through the motions, or understands the principles of skiing but never gets on the slopes, he or she can honestly say, "I know how to exercise" or, "I know how to ski." Actually doing it and reaping the benefits of the effort is another matter. In the same way, people often read books on religion and gain some knowledge of what spirituality means, but if that's all they do, they will acquire little feeling for the actual experience.

Hallowed be thy name. The phrase comes easily and is quoted often, but what does it mean? Even if we know the words, we can still be a long way from experiencing their significance. What does sensing the holiness of God's name feel like? *Hallowed be thy name* is about knowing God, not just with the head but with the heart.

As a small child, I sat in church, dangling my feet over the edge of the pew. In unison the congregation recited the Lord's Prayer. The word *hallowed* created in my mind an image of a hollow tree, and I wondered how God's name could be hollow or empty on the inside. Church school teachers chuckled at my association but were unable to give a satisfactory explanation of *hallowed*.

To Be Holy Is to Be Special

Not until years later did the significance of the phrase unfold. The word *hallowed* is taken from the word *hagios*, which means "holy." Literally, it means treating something as separate and special. A person is *hagios* when held in high regard, when regarded as separate or different from other people. For example, a wife relates with her husband differently, regarding him as more special than other men. To a husband, his wife is more special than other women. To a parent, a son or a daughter is more special than other children.

Something is *hagios* when it is regarded differently and held to be of more value than other things of its kind. A pressed rose is more than decaying matter to a woman who cherishes the memories associated with it. A child's kindergarten drawing, neatly fastened to the refrigerator door with a magnet, is more special to a mother than any masterpiece hung on the walls of an art gallery. *Hagios* is a highly subjective and deeply personal experience.

Originally, *hagios* had secular connotations such as those listed above. However, as usage matured, it assumed religious significance. Sunday, a day set apart from the rest of the week, is "holy" or *hagios* because it is designated for worship. A temple is "holy" or *hagios* because it is set aside for special services. An altar is "holy" or *hagios* because it is used differently than other pieces of furniture. The Bible is "holy" or *hagios* because it contains truths other books do not have. To hallow the name of God is to make it different and more valuable than other names and to regard it as holding special significance for our lives.

What is it, exactly, that we hallow when we pray the Lord's

Prayer? What's in God's name? In the Bible, a name is not just a label used to designate something, but a reference to the very essence of the thing named. Prophets often named their children to describe conditions pertaining to Israel. Thus Isaiah named his child "Speedy Booty, Speedy Prey." When Jesus changed the name of Simon to Peter (meaning "rock"), he attributed to him rock-like characteristics. It took years, with many setbacks, before Peter realized the significance hidden in his name.

To know the name of God is to know the quintessence of God. To hallow the name of God is to revere this essential nature, setting it apart from everything else and making it central in our lives. Psalm 20:7 reads,

> Some boast of chariots, and some of horses;
> but we boast of the *name* of the Lord our God.

In other words, while some put their faith in material things, those who hallow the name of God—that is, know the essential nature of the Divine—trust God to secure their lives.

Most people have a limited perspective on life, seeing the world in terms of what concerns them and taking everything else for granted. They are like field mice nibbling on grains of corn, oblivious to anything beyond the blades of grass and corn stalks that surround them.

Such people, while wrapped up in themselves, fail to hallow the name of God. The ego is either inflated or pernicious. On the one hand, people become puffed up with themselves. They look past their blessings—fine homes, rich food, a bounty of clothing—only to count their troubles and feel sorry for themselves. They wish they were in the mountains or at the beach, stretching one arm over the proverbial fence to grasp a handful of grass they believe is greener. On the other hand, people bathe in woe-is-me feelings, drawing all the attention they can from sickness or misfortune. Either way, pride limits life to an egocentric bubble of awareness.

God's name shines clearest for people who see life from a broader perspective. Spiritually sighted people have the capacity to transcend their egos. They understand wholes, systems, groups of things, and hallow the creative Power that manages it all. Unlike field mice bound to the earth, they are like eagles that soar over a wide range, aware of the whole terrain and sensitive to the slightest movement. They look between their bags of groceries and notice flowers growing in the cracks of the sidewalk. In a desert of concrete, small seeds find soil, grow, bloom, and announce to the whole world, *hallowed be thy name.*

People who pray the Lord's Prayer will notice a baby robin hopping on the ground and trying to fly. A nervous mother scurries about in nearby trees, trying to decoy any cat on the prowl. Soon the small bird flies, awkwardly at first but enough to find safety. And the mother robin darts off, singing in a language that only specially tuned ears can hear, *hallowed be thy name.*

In the early morning, people who hallow God's name will notice the sun painting the eastern sky to the glory of God or a meadowlark calling forth God's name from a nearby field. Late at night, they will see the full moon sprinkling diamonds that glitter on the surface of a quiet lake.

Having prayed the Lord's Prayer, if you peer into the spaces between things and listen to the silence between sounds, you will hear even the angels hallowing the ever-present name of God. *Hallowed be thy name* means being aware of God's authorship in every dimension of creation and sensing God's goodness woven through every event that occurs.

The English word *reverence* sums up the feeling of this petition. To pray *hallowed be thy name* means sensing a deep reverence for God and the sustaining power of God in every aspect of creation.

Learning About Holy Ground

When I was a youth on a Boy Scout campout, reverence became for me more than a word. While hiking in the Missouri woodlands, our patrol discovered an abandoned cemetery—small, overgrown with weeds, and surrounded by a wrought-iron fence. We climbed the fence and whiled away an hour or so reading the weathered tombstones. Some dated back to the eighteen hundreds. Most had epitaphs.

That night around the campfire we announced our discovery. The scoutmaster paused for a long moment before he said he hoped we didn't step on any graves. We all thought to ourselves, "Oops!"

The scoutmaster explained that this ground had been special to someone. At some time in the forgotten past, somebody brought flowers there to remember a loved one. Perhaps a widow returned often to one of those graves to be alone with her deceased husband. "That ground," announced the scoutmaster, "is hallowed."

Hallowed. Before, that word had been spoken only during worship when the congregation recited the Lord's Prayer. It was strange to hear it in reference to a patch of dirt. The next day I returned to the cemetery to examine the ground carefully. I climbed over the fence and wandered about the area, studying the earth and, this time, stepping over where I imagined someone was buried. Though I knew better, the scoutmaster's reverence for the ground gave me a childlike notion that something literal was there, something that made it special. Yet, it all looked the same. Everywhere the surface was covered with the same mat of dried leaves.

Being unable to distinguish sacred ground from any other ground implanted in me a seed, a thought that would one day mature. Now I remember, with the realization that all the ground around that cemetery was sacred—the trees that framed the place, the squirrels that scampered on nearby branches, the birds that kept the air alive with music.

Reverence, or hallowing God's name, means holding this kind of perspective. Instead of being locked into countless concerns of the moment, one attunes to God's nature and to the creative power of God in all events. God's name is active in each and every situation in which we find ourselves. To hallow God's name is to bring this reality into consciousness.

10. The Fullness of God's Kingdom

All things live and move and have their being in God's creative and sustaining power. By hallowing the name of God, you recognize this divine essence and know it as holy. If done correctly, this hallowing gives you more than an intellectual understanding of what the petition means. You have a deep and moving appreciation for who God is and what God does. This is the foundation of all prayer.

While the first petition is about knowing God, the second petition is about loving God. When you pray *thy kingdom come*, you bring the recognition of the first petition into your heart and thereby initiate the reign of God's power in your life. For a contemplative exercise that will enable this, use as a focus of concentration the phrase *thy kingdom come*.

God's kingdom is already a reality operating within each person. He or she may not be aware of it, however. By saying *thy kingdom come*, you recognize a state of being that already exists and bring it into full consciousness. It's like viewing a sunrise in which it only appears the sun is rising. Actually, the earth is turning toward the sun. With its dawning, God's kingdom appears as if it is coming. Hence, it is easy to think of it in this way. Actually, with the coming of God's kingdom, you are noticing a depth in your being that is perpetually present.

The two marks of awareness of God's kingdom are inner peace and outer harmony. Each depends on the other. Before there can be peace on earth, a substantial number of people must know peace within themselves. As peace comes to the earth, a greater number of people living within a peaceful world will be able to discover peace within themselves. Indeed, establishing inner peace through a closer union with God and a subsequent state of outer harmony among the communities of the world is one way to view the message and ministry of Christianity.

While I was at a wedding reception several years ago, I sat beside a proud grandmother. Anyone qualified for that role carries pictures of her grandchildren. This woman was overqualified.

She opened her purse and retrieved a string of pictures arranged in chronological order. Her eyes sparkled as she told the story of each child, beginning with her own daughters when they were babies. Each stage of growth was captured—their weddings, family outings, the birth of their children.

After fondling her memories, she paused. Her hands relaxed, falling limp in her lap. She gazed into space and with a sedate voice remarked, "My, my, how things do change."

I have often pondered her observation. Pictures are frozen memories. They allow us to look into our past and, in doing so, to be reminded of one inescapable law of life: how rapidly things change. Nothing can ever remain the same.

Life is swept along by shifting sands that constantly rearrange the terrain of our experience. One hardly has time to establish a footing. Amidst it all, we look for something solid, something permanent, something that is immune to the wear and tear of time.

We long for the good old days, remembering how things used to be when towns were small and people were friendly, when prices weren't so high and goods were made to last, when green tomatoes were placed in south windows and mother's homemade pie cooled on the kitchen window sill, when King David ruled Zion and Israel was at her zenith, when people obeyed the commandments and lived close to God. Back when . . . and so goes the cry.

We long for a better future, also, when our problems will be resolved and our responsibilities are lessened, when we earn our degree or have our book published, when our children are grown and the mortgage is paid and we can retire to the camper and travel at our leisure. We wish we were in Colorado on the ski slopes or in Florida on the beaches. We long for the return of a deceased loved one or another chance at a relationship gone sour. We long for a time when nations arbitrate peace and the lion lies down with the lamb. Someday, we muse, our Messiah will come and make things right. Then we will be happy. The the kingdom of God will reign, and there will be peace on earth and good will among all people. And, too, it will again be safe to walk the streets at night.

Every generation, in one way or another, looks to the past and then to the future, recalling how things were and fantasizing how things might be, and all the while saying to one another, "Someday!"

As we sit on our park benches, tossing bread crumbs to the pigeons and dreaming our lives away, a man appears, coming up a long and winding road. Even in the distance, his presence is commanding. We stop talking and stare. He looks a little like a prophet, robe and sandals and all. "He's from Nazareth," someone whispers.

This man walks up to us and studies our expressions. He knows what we've been thinking. He leans forward and whispers so softly that his words are almost inaudible, "There ain't going to be a someday. And there ain't no more good old days." He stands tall, spreads his hands wide, and shouts, "The kingdom of heaven is at hand. *This* is your life!" Then he leans forward again, places his hands on his knees, and whispers, "Any happiness you find, any peace of mind, any blessings bestowed by God, you must claim *now*."

Only in the here-and-now can we probe the depths and fullness of God's presence. Not in the future. Not in the past. Not somewhere else. The kingdom of heaven is now, right here, at hand.

This strange truth is an obvious but illusive fact. Who we are and what we have, right now, is all there is. Nothing can be other than what it is; and what is, exactly as it is, is God's reality for us. To deny what is, or dream it away, denies the very presence of God in our lives.

Grasping an understanding of the eternal present is one thing, but taking it seriously is quite another. People balk at the thought. "You mean right now? Right here?" With fixed incomes and tight budgets and persistent inflation and families in conflict and people living alone and birds that sing in the spring and squirrels that bury walnuts in the fall, this is all there is? Surely there's more! There ain't.

Indeed, the past is important, for it carries many lessons. But the past is an illusion that exists only in conjured memories. It is not a realm into which we can crawl to secure our happiness. The future, too, is important. It is critical that we dream and plan, for such is the essence of hope. But the future is equally illusive, for it exists only in our imagination. The future is not the realm where we realize inner peace. In the present moment, right now, hides the fullness of what it means to be a citizen in God's kingdom.

The kingdom of God is a theme central to the synoptic gospels. The parables of Jesus are woven around it and geared to shed light on its various aspects. The kingdom of God is like a mustard seed; the kingdom of God is like the pearl of great price; the kingdom of God is like a valuable treasure unearthed in a field; the kingdom of God is within.

God's kingdom can be understood as the inner peace derived from a conscious union with God and a corresponding sense of love that reaches out to the world around us. It is the very essence of what it means to love God with all our heart, mind, soul, and strength. We reach the realms of this kingdom through prayer and meditation.

An awareness of the ever present, fluid reality of God's kingdom must be renewed; this is why regularity in prayer and meditation is important. When we pray the Lord's Prayer, saying in the first petition *hallowed be thy name*, we make ourselves aware of God's creating and sustaining nature. This initiates a flow of thought in which we next pray *thy kingdom come*, insisting that our understanding of the divine essence be sensed in the innermost depths of hearts, here and now. By praying this petition regularly, we find that the kingdom of God is the single most important experience of our lives.

11. Yielding to God's Will

For a contemplative exercise promoting the ability to surrender to the will of Providence, follow the steps for prayer as outlined in chapter two while using for a focus the phrase *thy will be done*. Sense both the meaning of this phrase and its place in the Lord's Prayer. The feeling sought with this, the third petition, is one of surrender or letting go. It is a willingness to allow your will to align with God's and thereby to flow with the events that constitute life.

Within the Lord's Prayer, this petition completes the cycle designed to heal our separation from God. First, we recognized the nature of God and declared this nature sacred. Next, we sensed this divine nature as dwelling within our hearts and felt the inner peace associated with it. With this, the third petition, we seek to flow with God's indwelling power in every expression of our living. While the first petition is about knowing God and the second about loving God, the third is about following God.

As with the previous two petitions, consider the verb in this petition as passive. What you are affirming is a state of being, or better, a natural process of becoming. Indeed, God's will is being done in the natural course of things. Problems emerge when people fail to trust this process or try to hurry it along by insisting on their own way.

In our culture, the predominant story form finds expression in movies and television shows. Macho men, good guys with true grit and calm determination, confront bad guys flawed with arrogance and moral imperfection. The good guys always succeed by trusting their own cunning and skill. Beautiful women cheer from the sidelines as they resolve the dilemma. The bullets always miss, and the bad guys always lose. It's as if good and evil do not coexist in the same people.

Our society idealizes unrelenting willpower, true grit. Indeed, our country was built on it—hard work, necessary skills, and the determination to win. We train our children to compete, rewarding success in everything from football games to spelling contests.

Individual willpower can be a good thing. There is a sense in which survival depends on singular ability, as surely as any jungle animal lives by virtue of its strength and cunning. However, individual willpower and personal skill can be obstacles to surrendering to the will of God.

In my youth, I found a maple seed just beginning to take root. The sapling, less than two inches high, was the largest among several in the area. Carefully, I replanted it in a flower pot and took it home to nurse it along under the roof of our screened-in porch.

After a year or so, I said to my brother, "Look what I've grown."

My brother, always spoiling for an argument, replied, "Only God grows trees."

God, nothing. I was the one who watered it, protected it from the hard rains, kept the insects away, and gave it high-potency plant food. This was my tree.

One day I decided to return it to the wild. I took it to where I had found it and was amazed to find other saplings of its same age much healthier. Most were taller and had thicker trunks. It was as if God were saying to me, "Thank you very much, Ron, but I've been growing trees for quite some time now."

In much the same way, we confuse God's will with our own. God's will is considered something we can improve upon. All we need to do is take natural resources, or a natural state of affairs, and stir in it a little. We put enormous effort into our projects—designing them, gaining the necessary materials, implementing them. We assume that with self-determination and hard work, life comes together. After investing so much, we sometimes fail to recognize the force of Providence, which moves all things. In most cases, perhaps, things will turn out better if left alone.

To submit to God's will is difficult for two reasons. We often are confused about what exactly is God's will. And, once we understand God's intentions, our own will insists on doing battle with it.

Several years ago I purchased a stereo from a large department store. It came with a written guarantee that covered nearly everything—poor workmanship, faulty parts, etc. There was one disclaimer, however. It was not guaranteed against damages incurred as a result of "tornadoes, floods, hurricanes, and *other acts of God.*"

This represents a popular conception about the will of God. People believe God's will covers everything beyond human control—death and disaster, fate and fortune, good luck and bad. People joke about "lightning striking," and when the proverbial lightning does strike, they wonder what they did to deserve it.

What exactly is God's will? For Christians, the supreme revelation of God's will is the life, death, and resurrection of Jesus. God's will is this process in three stages. The life of Jesus is a witness to God's goodness. Jesus taught, by word and example, that God loves creation and will care for it. All we have to do is trust in God. Consider the birds of the air and the lilies of the field, Jesus taught, and know how thoroughly God cares for us. The first stage of God's will is goodness, growth, affirmation. It is anything that manifests the motherhood or fatherhood of God, the creative and sustaining power operating in life.

The death of Jesus is the contradiction of this innate goodness. The providential care on which Jesus counted didn't work for him, and he hung on the cross feeling forsaken. *Crucifixion* symbolizes the second stage in God's will. Always, there are times when God's loving goodness is contradicted and we end up being crucified in one way or another. We feel forsaken and hard pressed to understand the will of a loving God in the pattern of events. In every sector of life, there is a principle of crucifixion manifested in death, decay, suffering, and all endings.

One of the messages of the cross is that at any time you or I hurt, God also hurts. When Jesus died on the cross, it was God who bled, hurt, and suffered. And though God's will incorporates suffering, it is not that God wills us to suffer. Sometimes, when God's intent is frustrated, it is God who suffers in and through us so that through suffering, greater possibilities can be realized. This is the meaning of the third stage of God's will. The resurrection of Jesus is the ultimate resolution of the crucifixion principle. Through suffering, a greater good can be realized, if there is faith.

The *life*, *death*, and *resurrection* of Jesus is the paradigm of God's will wherever it is found. This triune process is an integral part of reality and represents the essential pattern of Providence: a process beginning with innate goodness, flowing through a contradiction of this goodness, and finding eventual resolution in a greater goodness.

It takes much experience, coupled with some quiet reflection, to know this triune process as more than just abstract theology. Once we experience it, however, we can begin to count on it.

Jesus challenged the religious authorities of his day while knowing the potential danger in doing so. Realizing the chances of being crucified, he retired to the Garden of Gethsemane to wrestle with his angel. There he expressed his desire for safety: "Remove this cup from me." However, he added to his prayer, "Not my will, but thine, be done" (Luke 22:42).

As we discern God's will as a concrete and even predictable process in day-to-day events, it becomes our task to surrender to God's will, trusting in its eventual outcome.

As long as our egos dominate the throne of our existence, God's will is an affront to our own. The primary way we enable the triune process of God's will is to enter our private Gethsemane and pray with Jesus, "Not my will, but thine, be done." This is probably the most difficult prayer anyone can offer.

Sometimes, yielding to God's will takes incredible courage. It means surrendering to the divine destiny embedded in all events, even when it means crucifixion. Faith in the resurrection is believing God's goodness will prevail in the long run.

An oak stands firm on a trunk that can be several feet in diameter. The grass growing in its shade is weak by comparison. Should a tornado strike, the oak may be torn away while the grass remains in intact. A subtle truth is suggested here. What yields and bounces back survives. What is rigid is often destroyed. To flow with the will of God means being spiritually resilient. When we pray the Lord's Prayer saying *thy will be done*, we are entering our Gethsemane and asking for the spiritual resilience to flow with the events of life, to be as pliable as grass bending in the wind.

This does not mean resignation, waving a white flag of surrender. Jesus was not wishy-washy in his approach to the forces that crucified him. Quite to the contrary, he took a strong stand. Yielding to God's will may mean risking, with reckless abandon, for what we believe is right. At the same time, it means laying our deeds on the altar of history and allowing God's will to work the magic.

The incredible truth is that, even when we make mistakes, God can take our errors and weave them into larger patterns of good if we are willing to surrender and flow with God's will.

Several decades ago, the strip mining that took place near Columbia, Missouri, plowed an ugly path northward, defacing many square miles and leaving large mounds of dirt beside deep gashes in the earth's surface. The mining company left the land as waste.

Nature has reclaimed the land. Trees and underbrush have matured, producing a rugged terrain and creating many hiding places for small animals. Hundreds of finger-like lakes curl through the area, providing habitat for fish and waterfowl. To capitalize in this natural beauty, the state set aside some of the acreage for a park.

Such is the fundamental spiritual law in God's universe. Responding to an innate wisdom, life is forever redeeming itself. If we can let go and flow with God's will, our own life will share in this redemptive process. Praying *thy will be done* enables this participation.

12. Our Daily Substance

No matter how spiritual one is, one has a daily need to meet material needs. God assures us that if we seek first God's kingdom, all needs are automatically met. For a spiritual exercise that will grant this assurance, practice contemplation using for a focus of concentration the phrase *Give us this day our daily bread.* Enter your prayer chapel, assume a comfortable posture, allow your breathing to settle, relax your body and assume a passive attitude; then repeat the phrase to yourself each time you exhale. You may wish to use a cadence of three, phrasing this petition with three breaths. Concentrate on the verb *Give* and on the image *bread.*

The word *bread* symbolizes everything essential for sustaining our lives. It represents the rich store of blessings from which we draw what we need and, in many cases, what we want. These exist and are real in a primordial or potential state. When saying the word *Give*, be aware of the abundant supply of provisions God makes available in this moment.

Consider the verbs in this and the next two petitions as active. Instead of recognizing a state of being, you want something to happen and are calling for an action. In keeping with the imperative mood of the verbs in the Lord's Prayer, seek to capture the feeling of manifesting a reality by declaring it so. Pronounce the word *Give* with insistence and a sense of expectancy. Feel the wanting; sense the need; call forth the blessing by the act of pronouncing the word.

We Begin by Trusting

As a pastor, I particularly enjoy the opportunity to visit new mothers in hospitals. After our visit, I walk down the hall to the nursery and put my nose against the glass. Some infants protest, testing new lungs. Others remain asleep.

Just home from the hospital, wrapped in a warm blanket and surrounded by everyone's love, a new baby locks its tiny hand around its mother's outstretched finger. Months go by, and the baby learns to hug. During the first year of its life (an extremely critical year for development), a baby works through the basic dynamics of trust and security.

As the infant grows older, instead of clinging to mother's finger, he or she hugs a teddy bear and will do so until the seams unravel and the stuffing flakes out. No other teddy bear will do.

Later, the child clings to toys and a host of objects scavenged from the yard and elsewhere that have little trouble stealing a child's interests. Children are natural collectors—rocks, miniature cars, Cabbage Patch dolls, baseball cards. As a youth, he or she will cling to a relationship or to an automobile fully polished and pampered.

Somewhere along the way, we lose our sense of primal security, so we cling to things that symbolize security—money, popularity, insurance policies. Throughout life, ownership is critically important. One of the three fundamental problems of human nature (as discussed in chapter three) is our tendency to form attachments for the sake of security. All human suffering can be traced, either directly or indirectly, to some form of attachment.

Before we can let go of our attachments, we must reclaim a sense of primal security. We do this not with more substitute gratifications, but with a silent knowledge that God will provide all of our needs on a daily basis if we ask for them in the spirit of the Lord's Prayer. We ask with the phrase *Give us this day our daily bread*. What we need will come to us as a matter of course.

When we fail to beseech God for our daily bread, subtle feelings of insecurity emerge in our lives. We are unable to sleep. Our bodies begin to break down with stress-related ailments. We cling to what we think will secure our lives. Given a little contemplative reflection, we will discover that such clinging is a result of losing touch with our primal need for security.

When we pray the Lord's Prayer and ask for our daily bread, we are asking for this primal sense of security, the silent knowledge that God is in heaven all is cared for in our world. Our peace of mind depends on this basic, inborn sense of security. Without it, life is filled with anxiety, despair, and even terror.

The Israelites Learned to Trust God

The Israelites knew despair after the Exodus. The security of Egypt was behind them. Their homeland seemed an impossible dream. Fortune had reduced their living to a sparse desert. How were they to build back lost faith?

As Moses led the people through the wilderness, God instructed them to gather manna from the land, only enough for one day's rations. Exceptions were made only when preparing for the Sabbath.

For forty years, the people had to believe that the next day's rations would be there. If they gathered a stockpile, it represented a loss of faith. It "bred worms and became foul" (Exod. 16:20). Quite possibly, it was this trusting that God's providential care would provide for them on a day-to-day basis that rebuilt their faith. Eventually, they came to believe they could indeed take the land God had promised. Our own faith is built by this same daily trusting that God will sustain our lives.

One day the prophet Elijah was hungry and appeared at the doorstep of a poor widow. She went to her jar of meal and shared some of her meager rations with him. Elijah blessed the woman so that as long as she lived, no matter how poor she became, there was always food in the jar. Any person who has confidence in God's infinite supply will always find his or her jar perpetually replenished.

Jesus was teaching the multitudes when it came time to eat. There wasn't enough food, so he took the five loaves and two fishes and blessed them, then divided them among the people. The supply was so great that the disciples didn't have enough baskets to gather the leftovers. The story is symbolic of how richly God will bless us when, in the spirit of the Lord's Prayer, we pray *Give us this day our daily bread*.

In the Sermon on the Mount, Jesus asks us to consider the birds of the air and the lilies of the field, how God cares for them. Animals and plants do not worry or squelch their life-energy trying to make ends meet. They simply enjoy the goodness and rich bounty God has provided. If we approach life with this same confidence, seeking first God's kingdom, all the things we need will come to us in the course of events.

Each petition of the Lord's Prayer makes possible all the others. We cannot begin our spiritual journey unless we recognize the creative nature of God in the world in which we live, hence we pray *Hallowed be thy name*. We cannot continue our spiritual journey unless we recognize this creative presence within our own lives, hence we pray *Thy kingdom come*. The task of the second petition is to make the recognition of God's nature (the essence of the first petition) a living reality within our hearts. Once we feel God's presence within us, we turn to the third petition to bring it out again, allowing God's will to find expression in our day-to-day living. By praying *Thy will be done*, we let go of our own will and completely surrender to the creative and sustaining power of God brought into our hearts with the first two petitions.

It is in this context that we pray for our daily bread. Without the first three petitions, we have no room in our hearts or time in our lives for God. We will be consumed with worry and anxiety over sustaining our existence. Praying the first three petitions of the Lord's Prayer grounds our consciousness in God and grants us a sense of primal security. This enables us to turn to the second half of the Lord's Prayer, beginning with the fourth petition. In a world beset by shortages, Christians sing a song of plenty: *Give us this day our daily bread.*

13. The Immediacy of Life

Living one day at a time is difficult. Using the fourth petition helps ground consciousness in the eternal presence and enables one to celebrate each day as it comes. Seated in your prayer chapel, relaxed and breathing deeply, become aware of all sensations *a la mode*, that is, the special way they are felt right now. Be aware of the sounds that filter into your consciousness. Feel the ground beneath you and the stillness of your posture. Attend to your breathing as it continues to slow and deepen. Sense the temporariness of each breath. Through it all, bask in the silent knowledge that what you need in this moment— air, warmth, nourishment, the support of the ground—is graciously provided.

To establish consciousness in the "here and now" of life, continue to use the phrase *Give us this day our daily bread*, concentrating on the words *this day* and *daily*. Each time your pronounce these words, feel the immediacy of the moment.

Your past is a collection of days. Has there been a day in which you've gone hungry or a week in which you were in want of shelter or the necessary clothing? The fact that you are alive now means that, in one way or another, your needs have been met.

The Endless Possibilities

Consider the birds that fill the air with music, the squirrels that scamper about in trees, and wild flowers decorating hillsides. Each species has a place in creation, a niche in which its needs are supplied in abundance. Misfortune may befall some within a species and bounty is enjoyed by others, but generally for each species the place in the ecological scheme of things is designed to be replete with bounty. The potential is there.

For each individual, in each moment, the possibilities fan out in countless directions. In praying *Give us this day our daily bread*, feel yourself reaching into the vast store of potentials and claiming the possibilities that exist for you right now in this very moment.

If you have done some of the spiritual exercises suggested to this point, you may have already cultivated a feeling for the immediacy of the moment. It is a concrete and tangible sensation that eludes words. It is a sense of "thereness," a consciousness of being "present."

Seek to feel this sense of inner peace and the accompanying sensation of immediacy at times other than those spent in prayer. Train yourself to claim it at various moments during the day, simply by taking a deep breath, holding it for a few seconds, and slowly letting go while relaxing and thinking a cue word like *shalom* or a phrase like *peace, be still*. Mastering this skill will eventually enable you to "pray without ceasing."

How sad things can turn out when people fail to claim the moment. I once knew a couple who were approaching retirement. They nurtured dreams of selling their home, buying a camper, and traveling about the country. They worked diligently for their dreams, each working long hours and putting in much overtime. They invested their earnings in bonds and purchased, from time to time, what they needed for their journeys—a large camper complete with microwave oven, color TV, and VCR.

The week before the husband's sixty-fifth birthday, he died of a heart attack. For years afterwards, their camper remained in the driveway, a monument to dreams unrealized. Each time I called, I walked past the full length of that camper to sit in the widow's living room and work with a grief process that stubbornly resisted resolution.

Our dreams and dreads of the future as well as regrets of our past can dampen our appreciation of the moment. We all have had experiences that pull us into the past. Maybe it is a missed opportunity. Maybe things were better in times gone by, and we sit in our rocking chairs staring out the window and musing about the "good old days." Maybe something happened in the past that offended us, and we can't get it out of our mind, so we go over the event, thinking of the things we could have said or done.

We also fantasize about the future. We dream of how things might be or scheme to make things better. Much time and effort can be spent on anticipating and preparing for things to come.

When I was nine years old, I could hardly wait until I turned thirteen, for then I'd be a full-fledged teenager. At thirteen, the magic age was sixteen. Then I could drive a car. At sixteen, my goal became twenty-one. Then the whole world would know I was an adult. Besides, I could vote. At age twenty-one, I looked forward to twenty-six. Then I'd be out of school (or so I thought) and have a family and be settled. I turned thirty during the time youth were reluctant to trust anyone so ancient, and I started looking back to my younger years. Now, well past forty, I've stopped counting.

Youth envies age, and age envies youth. The poor envy the rich, and the rich envy the richer. The tendency is to escape the complexities of life by wishing for what we do not have, or longing for a time other than now, or craving another place in which we imagine we could be happier.

Caught between the "no longer" and the "not yet," we are tempted to listen to the prophets of doom and run about like the proverbial chicken shouting "The sky is falling!" or to succumb to the intoxication of reminiscing and wishing life were somehow different.

All we need to do is look. The innocent faces of youth hold promises that things will always change. The wrinkled faces of death tell us that life does not go on forever. If we are locked in the past or anticipating the future, we are out of touch with inner peace, which can thrive only in the present moment. It seems to be a spiritual law: the only way to be at peace is to live one day at a time.

Living Totally in the Present

An emphasis on living one day at a time can be found throughout the scriptures and often occurs in passages dealing with the abundance of God's promised provisions. As was mentioned in the last chapter, when Moses led the Israelites through the wilderness, he instructed them to gather enough manna for each day, making exception only for the Sabbath. They had to believe the next day's supply would be there. By living one day at a time, they nurtured their faith until, eventually, they were able to take the Promised Land.

Jesus echoed this theme in the Sermon on the Mount, bidding us to consider the birds of the air and the lilies of the field. He concluded by saying, ". . . do not be anxious about tomorrow, for tomorrow will be anxious for itself. Let the day's own trouble be sufficient for the day" (Matt. 6:34). Again, the emphasis is on living one day at a time.

The Psalmist declared the glory of a single day.

> This is the day which the Lord has made;
> let us rejoice and be glad in it.
> Psalm 118:24

In one sense, the past and future are not real. The past is only our memories, and the future, our imaginings. Both memory and imagination are illusions of the mind and do not exist in the manifest world. The only reality there can be is in the present moment.

In another sense, the past and future exist mysteriously and concurrently in the present moment. Modern physics claims every past event and all future possibilities are concentrated in each progressive moment within multidimensional arrows of time. Reality is eternally *now*.

Living in the radical present, one day at a time, requires more than an intellectual grasp of an abstract truth. It requires an altered state of consciousness that is characterized by inner peace. Inner peace—like the exhilaration of skiing down a mountain slope, alive to the sensations of what is happening at each moment—is being able to relax and flow with the here and now.

One day while jogging on a path beside a river, I discovered a perfect metaphor. Anxious to cover the distance, I struggled along, digging at the ground ands pushing my stride with my arms. I was exhausted long before the finish line. Suddenly, a deer sprang from the bush, bounded across the path in front of me, and disappeared into the trees.

My awareness was yanked from its preoccupations and pinned to the present moment. I stopped thinking about how far I had come and the distance I had yet to cover. For a few precious moments, I heard birds singing and noticed butterflies fluttering about. Colors brightened and sounds became crisper. My stride lengthened, and my breathing settled into an even pattern. I felt as if I could run forever. "Runner's high" became more than something I read about in books. I sensed it. And I began to sense the contrast between moments like these and other moments preoccupied with the pressures and problems of living.

Consciousness plays in one of three arenas. When we are oriented toward the future, dreaming of some goal, or toward the past, wallowing in some resentment or basking in the glory of some achievement, we are engaged in "there and then" thinking. We lose a portion of our inner peace.

When we direct a multitude of dramatic daydreams or when we are preoccupied with abstract thought, analyzing and defining and criticizing, we are engaged in "this and that" thinking. Another portion of our inner peace wanes.

When we breathe slowly, relax, flow with events, and totally attune to each moment as it unfolds, we are in the "here and now." In such moments, an aura of peace will envelop us.

Life as we know it, right now, is all there is; and what's more, it's all we really need. What lies hidden in the present moment is the fullness of what God intends for us at this particular time in history and place on earth.

While leading a group of young people in a discussion, I asked them what they would do if they had but one week to live. Their ideas were fascinating and held one common denominator: each youth vowed he or she would live each day to the hilt. If only every day could be approached with this same enthusiasm! After all, life is but the sum of our days.

When we pray the Lord's Prayer and ask for our daily sustenance, we remind ourselves that it is only for today that we pray. Tomorrow, we will pray again. It is sufficient to find the fullness of God's blessings in the day, living just one moment at a time.

14. Our Forgiven State

Any obsession with the past blocks our inner peace. For a spiritual exercise that will clean the rust and debris we gather from living, use for a focus of concentration the phrase *Forgive us our debts*. The feeling sought with this petition is a freedom from the effects of past blunders and the sense of a fresh start.

Again, think of the verb as active. You are asking for something as opposed to recognizing a state of being. Feel the verb *Forgive* as imperative, and say the phrase with expectancy. You are insisting.

God's forgiveness is like a child's magic tablet purchased from the toy section of a department store. With a stylus, the child writes letters and draws pictures. When the child makes a mistake or grows tired of the drawing, he or she lifts the film-like sheet and the markings disappear. The surface is again unblemished, inviting new works of art. In every moment, we have this privilege of lifting a film and erasing the past, thus claiming a clean slate for a fresh start. We do so simply by declaring it so. This is the design of the petition *Forgive us our debts*.

The forgiveness of sin is a recurring theme throughout the Bible, particularly in the New Testament. The cup at the Eucharist signifies the blood of the new covenant poured out for forgiveness of sin. Jesus' death on the cross is understood as God's atonement, Jesus being the "Lamb of God" sacrificed for the expiation of sin. In Acts, the apostles taught that repentance for the forgiveness of sin is the prerequisite for the coming of the Holy Spirit.

What Is Sin?

As a child, I listened to ministers and teachers talk about forgiveness of "sins," and I wondered what I had done that was so bad. Sins were understood as bad behavior, and Jesus' death on the cross was somehow designed to make things right with God. It didn't make sense to me. Why would telling a few white lies or stealing a piece of candy from the supermarket demand such cosmic alterations in the divine scheme of things?

In saying the Lord's Prayer, what exactly is the debt for which we are asking forgiveness? What exactly is sin? To understand the Lord's Prayer, we must ask this question. Is sin misbehavior, or does it have more to do with temperament? Is the true nature of sin our misdeeds, or is it an inner condition that leads to misdeeds?

I believe it is most instructive to understand sin not as the wrong things we do *per se*, but as a poison within us from which springs the wrong things we do, a poison than can rob us of our happiness even if we do nothing wrong. Understanding sin more in terms of a faulty inner attitude and less as a tally of wrongdoings puts the petition *Forgive us our debts* in a different light. It is the poison within us that we are seeking to remove when we pray *Forgive us our debts.*

There were apple trees in the back yard where I grew up. In the summer when the apples were ripe, my brother and I were allowed to pick our choice. Sometimes it took several minutes searching the limbs for the biggest and shiniest apple. Often it required great effort, climbing through tangled branches, just to claim it. Then, while perched in the highest possible fork of the tree, I'd buff my apple against my T-shirt until it sparkled in the sun.

Only after I grew tired of anticipating the crunch and taste of sun-warmed cider did I bite into it. On more than one such an occasion, I found a fat worm inside, eating an ugly path through the core.

Sin is like a polished, worm-eaten apple. People can polish their characters by using the right tooth paste and the right soap, by dressing in the finest clothes. On the outside, they can sparkle in the sun, but inside, something extraneous to their nature eats away at their happiness.

Sin, the worm inside us. is pride. It is pretending to manage our lives by our own will, and thereby failing to yield to God's will. It is living out of an inordinate egocentricity and carrying the burden of responsibility for having so lived. Intoxicated with self-generated euphoria, people play God over their private kingdoms, and only when they look back and see in their wake a trail of unfulfilled or damaged lives do they get a hint that something might be wrong. They shudder at the thought that "I did it" or "I wasted it." How much easier it is to crawl behind the plea, "Someone else made me do it" or, "Circumstances left me no choice." Still, something inside knows better. People feel this something as a sense of being trapped by circumstances, or as a persistent and nagging string of regrets, or as a wishing that they had done something differently or that they could live part of their lives over again. Secretly, at some time or another, people beg fate to give them another chance.

What Is Forgiveness?

What does it mean to hear God pronounce forgiveness on such a human condition? Religious words such as *forgiveness* originate as metaphors. As time passes, such concepts tend to become metaphorically dead, rendering religious language dry and hard to understand. Religious creeds and rote prayers become clichés, giving us little or no awareness of the metaphoric vehicles that once gave them power and transformed human lives.

We can better understand religious terms if we grasp the metaphoric context in which they were born. One of the images behind "redemption," for example, is that of a slave market. An individual could purchase an enslaved relative and set him or her free. "Justification" has legal connotations and is associated with courts of law. Long accustomed to animal sacrifices, Jewish Christians understood Jesus as the "Lamb" of God. Giving gifts provided the background for the concept of God's grace. Paul may have thought about a Greek Olympic event when he wrote to a Christian congregation about "pressing on toward the goal" (Phil. 3:14).

The idea of forgiveness is taken from the practice of granting loans. Forgiveness implies a debt and a creditor wanting to foreclose. In a way, we put an impossible mortgage on our lives when we live out of inordinate egocentricity. In the process, we collect regrets — things we wish we had not said and things we wish we had done differently. We get behind on our payments, so to speak, keeping up pretenses while thinking about the past or holding ourselves back because we feel we don't deserve to get ahead. It all takes its toll. Something eventually has to break.

There comes a day of judgment when it all catches up with us. The balance is due and the creditor comes to foreclose. But instead of pushing us into bankruptcy, he refuses to collect.

Such is *forgiveness*. Divine forgiveness is standing before the heavenly judge, head bowed and our hands behind our backs. We hear the verdict read: guilty as charged. The sentence is that we spend a lifetime fretting and worrying over petty things, pursuits devoid of meaning, hassles linked to hassles, anxiety that becomes despair.

Then, as soon as the sentence is pronounced, we hear the good news—a pardon. The heavenly judge says, in effect, "It doesn't matter; I've integrated the past into a higher good. Go on with your life. Celebrate. Be free. Be at peace." And, we walk away free—free from the past and with a future wide open to new possibilities.

God's forgiveness, when deeply felt, heals all brokenness. One day while Jesus spoke to a large crowd, four men brought a paralytic to him. The crowds were so thick that their only option was to lower the paralytic through the roof of the house in which Jesus was standing. The stretcher came to rest at Jesus' feet. Jesus looked up and saw the faith of these friends, then said to the paralytic, "You sins are forgiven." Confusion spread through the crowd. Jesus went on to explain, "Which is easier to say, 'Your sins are forgiven' or 'Rise and walk'?" (Matt. 9:5). In this passage, Jesus equates forgiveness with healing.

Indeed, they are the same. This paralytic lived in a culture that taught that when people suffer, they are being punished for sin, either theirs or their parents', or maybe even their grandparents'. To hear that one's sins are forgiven meant there is no reason to continue suffering. One could pick up his or her bed and walk.

It seems inborn for people to carry feelings of guilt in the face of misfortune, even for people who are not particularly religious. Many times I have called on individuals in the hospital who reflect on their suffering with words like, "What have I done to deserve this?" Consciously or unconsciously, people connect ill-fate with a suspicion of moral failure.

God's forgiveness speaks to this deep, somewhat unconscious sense of responsibility to the world. At this level, God's forgiveness means a restoration of wholeness. When we realize, in the deepest part of our unconscious, that we are forgiven and that God loves us unconditionally—with a no-strings-attached-no-matter-what kind of love—then we have no reason to linger with the past or punish ourselves for some unreconciled problem. Not only are we free; we are healed.

God's forgiveness means we have the perpetual privilege of a fresh start. Imagine going to the beach early in the morning and being the first one there. We stroll out on the smooth and unblemished sand, then look over our shoulder to see our own footprints. Something inside us wonders if we really want to mar the scenery. Another part of us wants to leave our mark. We take a stick and scratch our name in the sand. By mid-afternoon, the beach is packed with people. By evening, it is a jumble of footprints, wrecked sand castles, and candy wrappers.

The derangement does not endure. Under the moonlight, there is an enforcement of the basic law of reality, namely, everything renews itself. The tide rolls in, and when morning comes, the beach is again smooth and unblemished. Our own lives are like this. Each moment is a new wave that smooths things out and allows us to start over. When we pray *Forgive us our debts*, we allow the waves of God's forgiveness to sweep over our hearts and remove our spiritual blemishes.

A river can carry the worst of pollutants, but if we stop the pollution and leave it alone for a few years, it will again run clean. In South America, people cut thousands of miles of dirt roads into the jungle. Travel on these roads is difficult because the jungle, as if it has a mind of its own, keeps reclaiming the land stolen from it. Nature is organized in such a way that everything renews itself. Destruction precedes new creation. Death hails new birth. Crucifixion summons resurrection.

Several years ago, a heavy storm buried our midwestern suburb. As in most northern suburbs, it seems, the deepest drifts stretched across driveways. I needed a clear path to remove my car and resigned myself to shoveling snow. As I cleared the driveway, I made a pile of snow off to one side. I enjoyed watching the pile grow to about seven or eight feet.

My daughter, preschool age at the time, watched from her bedroom window. She couldn't resist. Pretty soon, here she came with galoshes and gloves and an eagerness to play. She brought with her an old piece of cardboard for a sled and climbed on top of the snow mound. Then, perched on the summit on her piece of cardboard, she shouted, "Watch this, Daddy."

Because the slope was steep and she didn't start straight, her cardboard sled turned sideways and, about halfway down, she rolled and tumbled and splashed face down in the snow. Her performance was totally devoid of grace—about two on a scale of ten, and that only for her smile when she began. In spite of the mishap, she lifted her head up, snow clinging to her cheeks, and said, "Don't go away, Daddy. Let me try again."

Children are masters of this mysterious secret. They know life is a series of fresh starts. If they goof, it's their right and privilege to start again.

This is exactly what God's forgiveness is all about. It enables us to maintain our inner innocence. It guarantees renewed wholeness, no matter what our scarred past may be. It promises a succession of perpetual fresh starts. Forgiven by God, we know that if we make a mistake, or miss the mark, or don't quite reach the finish line, all we need do is admit it and try again. No guilt. No resentment.

In the Lord's Prayer, we claim this forgiveness by praying *Forgive us our debts*. In doing so, we remind ourselves of an ever-present truth. The pros and cons of the past are integrated into and ever-evolving goodness, and the future stands before us, wide open.

15. The Necessity of Forgiving Others

Probably the most difficult part of the Lord's Prayer is the petition that asks us to forgive others. Nothing blocks our sense of union with God more than harbored resentments. Yet, it seems, nothing is more difficult to resolve than these same resentments. A contemplative exercise which enables our forgiveness and which instills the attitude of forgiveness in the deepest recesses of consciousness is to concentrate on the second part of the forgiveness petition of the Lord's Prayer. In your prayer chapel—seated comfortably, breathing slowly, relaxed and passive—use for a focus of contemplation *as we forgive our debtors* or *as I forgive my debtors*.

Do not allow this phrase to become overly generalized. Capture specific situations and people to which it refers. Recall particularly, in the background of your repeating this phrase, people who have offended you and specific events that have damaged your life. Get a clear mental picture of these situations, allowing yourself to relive some of the emotions associated with them. Notice the tension these images create in your body.

As you say *as I forgive my debtors*, sense yourself forgiving specific individuals and events, each in turn. Feel your forgiveness of others coexistent with God's forgiveness of you. As you pronounce your forgiveness, feel your body relax and your inner peace swell within. To experience union with God, go over your past and forgive everyone and everything that has ever offended you.

It is a law of the mind that what is most troublesome emerges first. You will automatically recall people and events in the order of what bothers you most to what bothers you least. Allow the experience of forgiveness to unfold as if directed by a consciousness beyond yourself. Perhaps your awareness will return to something already covered. Allow it to do so, and again pronounce your forgiveness. Sometimes, you will symbolically envision offending people and events. Once, while doing this exercise, in the background of my saying *as I forgive my debtors* I visualized a white stallion on the Arizona desert rearing up and stomping at a rattlesnake. I allowed the drama to play itself out. Finally, the stallion stopped and drew its nose toward the snake. Also pacified, the snake touched its nose to the horse, then slithered into the rocks. I have no idea what this meant, but I remember the peace I felt when the war was over. Something in me had reconciled.

You may find yourself repeating your forgiveness phrase with nothing emerging in the background. At such times, you can deepen your experience of forgiveness by creating a symbol to represent all offending people and events that may be hiding from your consciousness. On one occasion, I pictured a blackboard with ugly markings on it. I erased the markings each time I pronounced the phrase *as we forgive our debtors.*

The phrase *as we forgive our debtors* is the only part of the Lord's Prayer that asks something from us. Everywhere else, we either recognize some aspect of God's rule or ask something from God, depending on whether we use the verbs in the Lord's Prayer as passive or active. The second half of the forgiveness petition is a critical point in the whole prayer, for it introduces an element of contingency. Whether we forgive others determines how effective the rest of our prayers will be.

The depth of your inner peace is directly proportionate to your ability to forgive the past. Yet, of all issues in spiritual growth, this is probably the most difficult. Of all the contemplative exercises involving the Lord's Prayer, this will perhaps be the most demanding.

Letting Go of the Past

During a lecture to a group of single people, I posed the question, "Does forgiveness mean forgetting?" One man, seemingly bitter about his divorce, said, "No, we must remember." He shared his reasoning: "We remember so we won't get hurt the same way again."

A mother of two teenage girls, having lost her husband in an automobile accident and struggling to make ends meet, said, "Yes, we must forget." She continued, "We must let go of the past so we can get on with living."

What stands out in my memory of that evening with this singles group is a conversation I had afterward with a divorced woman, She spoke in detail about her alcoholic ex-husband. She related how he had left her with three children, how she lived on welfare until she found a job, how she struggled to keep her children in school. As she spoke, her fists clenched and her eyes fluttered to hold back tears. I asked her how long she had been single. "Nine years," she replied.

While I mingled in the group, others who saw me talking with this woman said things like, "Oh, you heard her story, too" and, "She's told that story a thousand times." How sad, I thought, to hold a grudge for nine years, allowing it to fester, constantly turning it over in the mind, never letting go. Telling her story, relishing the hurt, venting her anger—all had become not a way of working through the problem but a way of relating. Admittedly, the pain had been great, but what a waste of precious happiness to still be reliving it after nine years.

In one way or another, all people struggle with forgiveness. Even in the best of marriages, forgiveness is needed. It is not easy for two people, raised in different ways, to come together and make a marriage work. To remain happy, married couples must learn to forgive their partners.

Children, no matter how loving their relationship with their parents, carry hurts that can be healed only with forgiveness. Even grown-up children—and grown-old children—have ghosts from their childhood that refuse to die. These ghosts intrude upon their lives, crowd out spontaneity, and find ways of acting out their peculiar quirks. The only way to disarm a ghost is to forgive it.

Parents love their children, but there are times when they do not like them. Sometimes, infants are less than cute, and children are not simply irritating but downright obnoxious. Youth, in making their emancipation proclamation, can be offensive and hard to understand. Again, forgiveness is necessary.

Why It's Hard to Forgive

Feelings of resentment are not always rational. When reasons cannot justify them, people often feel guilty for feeling resentment. Sometimes, widows and widowers need to forgive a departed loved one for dying and leaving them alone. Being unable to understand such a strange need for forgiveness, they end up feeling sorry for themselves.

Life doesn't always play fair, and often there is no one to blame except God. Being unable to forgive God, consciously or unconsciously, can leave a person cynical. If such persons, like the Psalmist, could shake a fist at heaven, even forgiving God is possible.

In a Bible study, I asked the group if God were to grant them one free punch, how many knew of someone they would like to poke. With some humor, they used their imagination and every hand went up, including my own. As the discussion continued, it became apparent that everyone, in one way or another, was struggling with forgiveness.

Why is it difficult to let go of an offense? The difficulty of forgiveness is fourfold, involving the frequency of an offense, its intensity, our insistence on fairness, and our inclination for recollection.

(1) *Frequency.* Most people can forgive an offense once, maybe twice. After a third time, the pace of forgiveness becomes tiring.

Picture, if you will, Jesus approaching his disciples and finding Peter with his hands in his pockets, kicking at the dust. "What's wrong, Peter?" Jesus asks.

"It's about this idea of forgiveness," Peter protests. "I mean. it's a good idea and all, but how often do we have to keep doing it?" Peter gives a liberal option: "Maybe as many as seven times?"

We can identify with Peter. Forgiveness is a demanding rule. Forgiving once leaves us feeling righteous. We can forgive even twice and keep some sense of propriety. After a third time, it starts becoming uncomfortable. It seems we're getting nowhere. If we manage to hold onto our composure and forgive as many as seven times, what an accomplishment! That would make us outstanding spiritual athletes.

Imagine the sense of defeat, as well as awe, when Jesus told Peter that if he must keep score, make the number seven times seventy. People will not keep that kind of tally long before discovering something. Forgiveness, at least the kind Jesus advocated, is not an occasional shift in attitude but a perpetual disposition of character.

(2) *Intensity.* Most people can forgive little things. Some things, however, seem too big and the hurt too deep to forgive.

In the Old Testament, justifiable revenge was an acceptable solution for human injustices. An eye for an eye and a tooth for a tooth— so goes the saying. When Jesus taught the need for forgiveness, people found it troublesome. Though the truth of forgiveness was traditional and even philosophically palatable, the practicalities were difficult to realize.

To make forgiveness work required a new understanding of God. It meant seeing God as one whose primary nature is love—not as one characteristic among others, but of the very essence of the Creative Force. Jesus advocated this understanding and carried it to the cross, grounding it in history with his dying breath. He said of the soldiers gambling at his feet, "Father, forgive them; for they know not what they do" (Luke 23:34).

Anyone who would stand in the shadow of the cross can do no less. There is absolutely nothing so overwhelming that it cannot be forgiven.

(3) *Fairness.* Most of us, when we hear the story of the prodigal son, identify with the forgiving father. He is the one the story is about. However, when we experience the injustices of life, we feel more like the older son who stayed home and worked hard while his younger brother was out living it up. It wasn't fair for his brother to receive the warm reception and the party in his honor.

People have an inborn expectation that life will play fair. Imagine two brothers scuffling on the living room floor. One accidentally hits the other. The one hit feels a need to get even, so he strikes back. The first brother, knowing his blow was accidental and not deserving of retaliation, strikes again, just to even the score.

Finally, the mother enters the room and asks, "What's going on?"

"He hit me!"

"Well, he hit me first."

The mother places her hands on her hips and says, "Go to your rooms!"

In chorus, the boys cry out, "But that's not fair!"

In like manner, we want to keep things even. When life is unjust, we too cry out to the Father in heaven, "But that's not fair!" At one time or another, these words linger on the lips of all of us.

When they do, we suffer from a Jonah complex. We demand repentance from our enemies and pronounce God's forgiveness on those who offend us, but inside we smile at the thought, "God will get them for that!" The idea that God might forgive our enemies, allowing them to get off without smarting for the pain they've inflicted on us, just doesn't seem fair.

"Crime does not pay"—so we've been taught. "There will be a time of reckoning," preachers have said. And though the rain falls on the just and the unjust alike, it's comforting when the balance is in our favor.

We like the idea of God forgiving us for our shortcomings. This is God's grace, a display of God's mercy. But in our heart of hearts, when someone offends us, we're not so sure we want God to forgive them. That ruptures our sense of fairness by planting a big question mark on the whole scheme of rewards and punishments.

When we balance our checkbooks, what comes out must match what goes in. Likewise, we want to believe people withdraw from life what they deposit. If we allow our honesty to transcend our religious platitudes, taking the idea of forgiveness seriously is offensive. It means accounts are perpetually unbalanced in the bank's favor.

To pray sincerely *as we forgive our debtors* is extremely difficult. We can bow our heads and take comfort in saying *Forgive us our debts*, but we choke when we realize what it means to pray *as we forgive our debtors*. It takes great effort, working diligently with ourselves, to master this single phrase. Yet, our inner peace depends on it.

(4) *Recollection.* Does forgiveness mean forgetting? Yes and no. No, in the sense that we learn from experience. If a rattlesnake bites, it's important to remember the sound of the rattle. Memories teach us to be careful.

And yes, forgiveness means forgetting in the sense that no one can drive into the future with his or her eyes glued to the rearview mirror. It's like saddling a donkey backward, preferring to see where we've been rather than where we're going.

The lesson of Lot's wife is forever true—to lock our gaze on the past is paralyzing. Jesus made this point when he said, "No one who puts his hand to the plow and looks back is fit for the kingdom of God" (Luke 9:62).

Forgetting is the primary difficulty with forgiveness. Sometimes people have righteous intentions, but the experience of being offended keeps popping into their minds.

For our peace of mind, it is critical that we find closure on the past. Resentment always hurts the resenter more than the resented. Before we can have peace with God, we must first make peace with those around us, including our greatest and most love-defying enemies.

But how? By praying the Lord's Prayer. We let go of the past by calling the offending person or situation to mind, with all its emotional ramifications, and consciously pronounce the forgiveness phrase *as we forgive our debtors*.

How Can We Forgive?

Forgiveness means three things: (1) finding closure on a painful past, (2) understanding God's providential plan in forgiveness, and (3) disconnecting ourselves from the hurt so we can refocus the mind.

(1) *Finding closure on a painful past.* Once, while driving along a country route, I saw a squirrel scamper across the road. When I drew closer, I discovered it was a paper sack caught in the wind. Why did I, at first, see the squirrel? The mind wants to complete things. Psychologists call this a tendency for closure. My mind had picked up a few clues and created a mental picture of a squirrel by closing in the details. It grasped a few lines and shapes, then formed what it thought it saw. Only when I drew closer and more details were available did my mind make the correction with a different mental picture.

What is true with spatial relationships is also true with time and sequence. Situations also demand closure. When something is unfinished, our minds seek completion. More than once have I sat through a meeting in which there was something I wanted to say, something contrary to the prevailing opinion. At one meeting in particular, I held back, feeling that if I said what I wanted to, it would be inappropriate. On the way home, my knuckles turned white as I gripped the steering wheel and gave my best speech to the road ahead. What was unfinished lingered in my mind, seeking completion.

At the breakfast table, a husband and wife have an argument. Each go their respective ways. Throughout the day, each dwells on the argument, reviewing what was said and rehearsing what he or she would have liked to have said.

Reviewing and rehearsing new sequences for a past situation is the mind's way of seeking closure. With images, thoughts, and emotions, it relives the situation, struggling to find a solution and, all the while, keeping us out of touch with the eternal present and the inner peace it holds.

This is precisely the problem of forgiveness. When our minds dwell on an offending person or situation, we are seeking a resolution by rehearsing the variety of ways we might have "gotten even," or "completed," or "finished," or "closed out" the offending event. Try as we may, we can't quit thinking about it, and sometimes we will compulsively talk about it. At night we may dream about it. For years, even decades, our minds can persist in the effort to resolve an offense if it has been left unfinished.

What complicates the matter is that the body physiologically reacts to the contents of the mind regardless of whether or not they are real. This truth is easy to prove. Think of a lemon. Picture it, and mentally feel its texture. Notice the pores and the bright yellow of the skin. Visualize slicing it with a sharp life, and feel the spray against your cheeks. Bite into it and feel the juice ooze around your teeth. You may notice your jaws tingling. All this, and no lemon is actually present. The physical reaction is caused by the passive acceptance of a visualization in your mind.

Rehearsing things we would like to have said or done, reliving hurts, and savoring the grinding pleasure of getting even—all take their toll on our bodies. They keep us tense and upset. The inability to let go of the past and go on with living can literally make us sick.

It is next to impossible to remove an unfinished situation from the mind. We can only succeed in pushing it our of consciousness. In the unconscious, it still lives and cries out from unfelt depths for resolution. Such hidden conflicts poison our happiness Is any enemy or past offense worth the price that it exacts from our lives?

The problem of forgiveness is a problem of finding closure. Instead of trying to put the painful experience out of mind, we will find it more helpful to establish the closure we are seeking.

One very effective way of doing this was outlined in the opening of this chapter. While contemplating the phrase *as we forgive our debtors*, as vividly as you can visualize them, allow the persons and events that have offended you to emerge in your consciousness. For a moment, cease saying the phrase and relive the hurt. Feel it, and notice where tensions form in your body. Experience the painful situation, and then voice your forgiveness with the phrase *as we forgive our debtors*.

Allow the experience to dissipate as if a fog rolls in, consumes your mental imagery, and soothes the tensions out of your body. Objectify, allowing the distance to grow between you and your image of the offense. As the experience moves farther and farther away, continue pronouncing your forgiving phrase *as we forgive our debtors*.

Your mental imagery will adjust according to the sincerity of your forgiveness. Perhaps the images of painful situations will evaporate as water on a hot sidewalk or disappear as a thick fog rolls in and swallows them. As these images lose their intensity, the emotional charge they carry will drain away and be replaced with a pervasive sense of inner peace.

(2) *Understanding God's providential plan.* Once upon a time, a man looked with keen eyes down a long dusty road and saw a group

of men slowly making their way to his palace. Something about this group, something in the way they walked and rode their donkeys, seemed strangely familiar. Hebrews; they were from up north.

Slowly, memories began to emerge, bad memories from a time long forgotten, memories that enabled him to recognize these men as his brothers. They had beaten him and had thrown him in a pit. Later, they had sold him as a slave to a caravan going to Egypt. While living within his memories, he could feel the heat coming up from the sand as he rode the back of that camel on the hot and endless desert.

After suffering the humiliation of the auction block, he struggled to live amidst a people whose language he hardly understood. Then there was that incident in Potiphar's house where he was wrongly accused of having an affair with Potiphar's wife. He spent two long years in prison because of a false accusation. Long nights they were, with dirt and filth and empty dreams of a little boy wearing a multi-colored robe and running free outside his father's tent.

All this suffering was because of the thoughtless brutality of these men who were now coming to visit him. Can you imagine the resentment, the images of revenge, Joseph must have felt as he watched his brothers coming to Egypt?

The tables were turned. Famine had struck the land, and these brothers were soon to be on their knees before Joseph, begging for a handout. God had raised Joseph from slavery and the prison cell to make him chief assistant to the Pharaoh. As the Psalmist would later recount, God had delivered his enemies into his hands, making them a footstool for his feet. Just think of the fury he could have unleashed. And who would have blamed him? After all, it would have been fair.

The story of Joseph reveals a cautious man with a compassionate heart, capable of forgiving his past and, through his capacity to forgive, able to save his people. What is significant about the story of Joseph is not just that he forgave his brothers, but his reasoning for it. "Don't feel bad," he said, in effect, "You meant it for evil, but God had a different plan." The Jerusalem Bible translates it this way: "The evil you planned to do me has by God's design been turned to good" (Gen. 50:20, JB).

This important, all-embracing principle is nothing less than the crucifixion-resurrection paradigm, which works the same way in our own lives. If we forgive, God can take the offense and weave it into a larger pattern of good. This is the miracle of forgiveness, and we release this miracle every time we forgive. Indeed, whether divine or human, forgiveness is the energy of resurrection.

In a strange sense, people who offend us do us a favor. Paul knew this when he wrote in Romans 5:3-5, "We rejoice in our sufferings, knowing that suffering produces endurance, and endurance produces character, and character produces hope, and hope does not disappoint us, because God's love has been poured into our hearts through the Holy Spirit which has been given to us." All this because God takes the raw material of broken circumstances and rebuilds new and more substantial lives, if we simply allow it and do so with our forgiveness.

(3) *Disconnecting ourselves and refocusing.* In addition to letting go of the past, forgiveness means getting on with living.

The church at Corinth had serious internal problems. A certain individual was stirring up trouble. When Paul visited Corinth, this man, the leader of some form of opposition, criticized him, infecting the whole church with discontent. "Someone has been the cause of pain . . . not to me, but . . . to you all," Paul wrote (2 Cor. 2:5, JB).

The church took action against the troublemaker, and their political problems were solved. However, they discovered they faced a more serious spiritual problem. Some wanted revenge. After all, this man nearly wrecked the church.

At this point, Paul asked the church at Corinth to be compassionate. The problem had been resolved. Now was the time for forgiveness, a letting go of the past and getting on with the building of new life.

Like the Corinthians, many religious people are inclined to seek punishment for offenders—in the name of justice, of course—as if to help God get even. Recognizing that vengeance belongs to God, Paul suggests that once a situation is corrected, we are not to waste our spiritual energies wallowing in thoughts of revenge. We are to let go and get on with living.

It's easy to look down a long bony finger that points to someone else and ignore the three fingers pointing back at us. These three fingers are perhaps symbolic. What begins as someone else's problem soon becomes triple our own. Being unwilling to forgive causes ugly scars to form on our spiritual countenance. And we are often blind to the reasons why, since it is more soothing for the ego to believe that someone else "causes" our suffering. We are slow to admit that we perpetuate our own pain.

When we point at someone else's faults we are like a movie projector that casts an image on a screen. Everyone looks at the screen to see who is to blame. Only as we study the process do we realize that the picture is projected from within ourselves. What we resent in others seems to be "out there." In actuality, it is a shadowy reflection of our own inner world.

No one, upon examining his or her heart, can cast the first stone. The very thing we try to extinguish is visible precisely because it is a projection. Paul is unmistakably clear about this: "Therefore you have no excuse, O man, whoever you are, when you judge another; for in passing judgment upon him you condemn yourself, because you, the judge, are doing the very same things" (Rom. 2:1).

The cause of our suffering is not in people or situations outside ourselves, but in our identification with those people or situations. We are emotionally attached to them.

If we could take our anger out and look at it, we would see how ugly it really is. And we would see how much it cripples our lives. Our healing begins when we disconnect ourselves from those people and situations that "cause" us pain. Part of what helps us do this is realizing the problem is indeed ours and not theirs.

In addition to disconnecting, we need to refocus our mind. The world is a rich and fascinating place, and the joys of inner peace are beyond comprehension. Clinging to a past is not worth what we stand to miss. Saying *as we forgive our debtors* enables us to let go and get on with living.

The dual petition—*Forgive us our debts as we forgive our debtors*—is a microcosm of the whole Lord's Prayer. It carries the same twofold structure. *Forgive us our debts* reflects the vertical dimension of the first three petitions and concentrates on healing our separation from God. This vertical reconciliation forms the basis of the horizontal dimension, which heals our alienation from others. We manifest the healing by praying *as we forgive our debtors*.

While the phrase *Forgive us our debts* builds the foundation for *as we forgive our debtors*, the latter phrase ratifies the former. We cannot have peace with God unless we first sense our harmony with others. This includes loving our most hard-to-love enemy.

In a sense, when we pray *Forgive us our debts as we forgive our debtors*, we are asking God to forgive us exactly as we forgive others. The additional commentary Jesus adds after giving the Lord's Prayer—the only part of the prayer that receives further comment—suggests that God's forgiveness of us is indeed modeled upon our forgiveness of others (Matt. 6:14–15). If we ask God to pattern his forgiveness of us after the way we forgive others, we have the heavy responsibility of making our forgiveness of others as perfect as possible.

The contingencies attached to God's forgiveness of us are not because God withholds forgiveness until we meet God's conditions. It is the nature of reality that, before we can be receptive to God's forgiveness, we must clean our hearts of all our resentments toward others. There is nothing noble or pious about forgiving our enemies. For the sake of inner peace, it is only practical.

16. Life's Testings

For one set on a spiritual journey, life will not always be filled with inner peace, and there will be times when ill will prevails among people. The Lord's Prayer makes provisions for such times. For a contemplative exercise that will strengthen us during such times, use for a focus of concentration the phrase *Leave me not in my trials* or the collective form *Leave us not in our trials*. Notice that the suggested wording of this petition varies from the traditional form. This will be explained later.

Alternative phrases might include: *Leave me not while I am tested, Leave us not in the midst of our testings, Leave me not in temptation,* or *Leave us not in temptation.* The wording is not as important as the sense of meaning derived from it.

The petition may be used to capture the assurance of God's guidance through the complex maze of life's events. It is a sense of God's continued presence in situations that test our faith.

In my opinion, the above translations, variations from the familiar version, capture a truer sense of this meaning. The popular translation *Lead us not into temptation* suggests that God might tempt us. Other passages in scripture indicate that this is impossible.

Enter your prayer chapel, assume a comfortable posture, and allow your breathing to settle. Relax your body and assume a positive attitude. Then, each time you exhale, pronounce the phrase *Leave me not in my trials* or one of the variations of the above. Sink into a feeling of God's perpetual presence.

Actually, God never leaves us. When life becomes difficult, we sometimes rely on our own means to solve problems. In such moments, we lose our awareness of God's presence and guiding power. It feels as if God has left us when, in reality, we have only lost our awareness of God.

When we pray *Leave us not in our trials*, we are not as much asking for God to stay with us as we are reminding ourselves that God is always with us. We are encouraging our awareness to stay with God during the difficult moments.

As with the last two petitions, consider the verb active. Instead of recognizing a state of being, you are asking for something to happen. You want God's presence to shine through the sometimes too demanding claims the world makes on your awareness.

The last two petitions focused on the present (our daily bread) and the past (our debts and those of others). This petition anticipates future moments of difficulty. When we realize inner peace in a moment of contemplation, that is not a moment in which we are being tested. In that moment, we are immune to the devastation that can result from the pressures of the world. The temptations referred to in this petition lie ahead.

A Better Translation of This Phrase

Though not difficult to pray sincerely, this petition of the Lord's Prayer is, for many people, the most difficult to understand. The popular translation of this petition—*Lead us not into temptation*—is confusing. It implies that God might lead us into temptation and, to prevent it, we ask God not to. God does not plan entrapment. James 1:13 says, "Let no one say when he is tempted, 'I am tempted by God'; for God cannot be tempted with evil, and he himself tempts no one; but each person is tempted when he is lured and enticed by his own desire."

The Aramaic version of the Lord's Prayer, popular in Eastern Christianity, informs our understanding of the prayer in ways our western translations are lacking. For me, the greatest contribution from the Aramaic version is with this petition. A loose and amplified paraphrase of the Aramaic version might be: *Keep us from entering the arenas in which we are tempted and stay with us should we, by our own errors or the injustices inflicted by others, find ourselves tested in those arenas*. There is a twofold flavor in the ideas presented in this rendering. This petition and a semblance to the familiar form is captured in a simplified translation of the Aramaic: *Leave us not in temptation* or *Leave us not in our trials.*

Three implications in this rendering struggle to leap over the translation barrier and convey their meaning. The first, carried in the phrase "Leave us not," implies "Stay with us." Jesus felt forsaken when he hung from the cross, as we do when in the midst of our crucifixions. We feel abandoned and need to cry out to God, "Don't leave us in this mess! Stay with us!" Praying this phrase in the Lord's Prayer prepares our hearts and minds for those situations that will test us. It conditions us to be open to that Power which is beyond our own understanding and our own will.

A second concept buried in the middle of the phrase *Leave us not in temptation* may be glossed over. When tested, we struggle within a context or arena. The word *in* or the phrase *in the midst of* conveys the picture of such an arena.

The third concept carried in this phrase *Leave us not in temptation* is the complex idea of temptation itself. This concept has several connotations that together shape its meaning and strain any single-word rendering. One connotation is the notion of *seduction*. This is normally what we associate with temptation—an enticement to do wrong.

James 1:14 states that "each person is tempted when he is lured and enticed by his own desire." This implies that the real source of seduction is not the seducer but the desires in the heart of the seduced. In a real sense, it is protection from ourselves that we seek when we pray *Leave us not in temptation.*

A story by Mary Howitt, set to poetry over a century ago, describes temptation understood as seduction. A spider tried to entice a fly into his parlor. He tried many ploys—pretty things to show the fly, a place to rest, fine food. Finally, the spider admires the fly's brilliant eyes and gauzy wings and offers it a mirror so that it might behold itself. In time, the fly returns to meet its doom. The spider's role is secondary. The fundamental cause of the fly's demise is its vanity and the desires of its own ego.

So it is with temptation. The mechanism that springs the trap is the vanity and desires of our own ego. When we pray this phrase in the Lord's Prayer, we are asking God to protect us in those places within which we are vulnerable to ourselves.

Another connotation buried in the word temptation is the idea of *worldliness.* We are tempted not by worldliness itself, but when we are consumed by the cares of the material world. Again, what makes it temptation is the tendency, when so consumed, to forget God and rely on our own resources to make our lives secure. When we pray *Leave me not in temptation*, we are asking for the strength to guard against being seduced by the concerns of the world.

This does not mean that we give up materialism. The world and all its goodness is God's gift to us. This petition helps prevent us from being so obsessed with the benefits and problems of living in the world that we forget the power of God at work in all situations. When we pray this phrase, we seek not to forget God in moments of pain and pleasure.

Another and more common connotation in the word temptation is *testing*. We think of a test as a way of proving who we are, what we know, or what we can do. Indeed, in the Bible, the concept is used in this way. Before Joseph welcomed his brothers into Egypt, he tested them by threatening the life of Benjamin. Only when they showed compassion did Joseph reveal himself to them. Gideon tested his men before doing battle with the Midianites, selecting for his army those who lapped water watchfully, like dogs. Only three hundred men passed the test, but with them God won victory.

Testing, however, not only proves the mettle of faith; it often refines and shapes and hones it. Before Jacob was reconciled with his brother Esau, he wrestled with the angel. The process of wrestling enabled him to grow.

When Abraham migrated into Canaan, he moved into a culture where people sacrificed their first-born sons to the fiery god, Moloch. Abraham felt it his religious duty to sacrifice his only son, Isaac. Wrestling with this expectation provided the classic test of faith. He emerged from the struggle with a new understanding of God, one that became the foundation of three of the world's major religions: Judaism, Christianity, and Islam. Abraham's innovative approach to religion grew out of this testing.

Job was tested when he lost everything. In his grief, three friends came to help him struggle with the reasons why. The experience was grueling, but from the other side of the whirlwind, Job emerged with a profound humility that enabled him to reclaim his health and prosperity. The strength of his newborn faith, one that trusted the mystery of God more than any rationale as to why things happen the way they do, was made possible by his experience of being tested.

At some time in our lives, each of us will find ourselves tested. During these times, not only will our true character emerge, but the very process will develop our faith in ways otherwise impossible. Our struggles, if we allow them to, will temper our spirits and make us stronger.

God will give us the power and wisdom to prevail in our testings, just as God answered the prayer of Jesus in the garden. God didn't remove the cross from Jesus, as he requested, but gave him strength to go through with it.

No test will ever be too big for us, and every test will have within it both a way through and benefits to be realized. Praying the petition *Leave us not in our trials* grants us these two things. One is the guidance through the maze of events that will test us. The other is the strength and wisdom to claim the goodness made available by the testing itself.

17. Overcoming the Fundamental Human Flaws

Evil, the absence of God in the course of events, is generated from several sources. It can originate from within each person, spawning out of egocentric pride, alienation, or idolatry. It can be experienced as injustice or violence inflicted by individuals on other people. It can come from forces larger than individuals, such as the oppression of institutions and the collective consciousness of entire societies. Evil is any manifestation in the world in which the consciousness behind such manifestations is self-centered, that is, when it lacks a universal spiritual awareness.

There are times when we are victims of evil, either the evil generated out of ourselves or evil forces larger than ourselves. For a contemplative exercise that will inoculate us from evil, use for a focus of concentration the phrase *Deliver us from evil* or the personal form *Deliver me from evil*. In your prayer chapel, sitting quietly and breathing gently, silently pronounce the phrase each time you exhale. Think the phrase as you would any thought passing through your mind, attending to the sounds and allowing the meaning to soak in. Without your effort, this phrase will address the deeper parts of your consciousness of its own accord.

Deliver us from evil is an extension of the first half of the petition *Leave us not in temptation*. In the first half, we ask God to stay with us when we are being tested. In the second half, we recognize the forces against which we struggle in our moments of testing and ask for deliverance from them.

To pray *Deliver us from evil* requires an understanding of two concepts, "deliverance" and "evil." The concept *deliverance* combines the the notion of being separated from something (as wheat is separated from chaff) and the idea of being set free (as an animal is released from a cage). *Deliverance from evil* means God disassociates us from it and frees us from its influence. As you pray this phrase, feel the deliverance.

Where there is racism, or sexism, or ageism, feel that God is removing you from these processes. Where there is consumerism—an inordinate need to consume or own or control things and people—hear God's word denounce the demonic. Where there is inordinate class-consciousness and injustice and war, join God's will in renouncing the subtle invitations and social pressures to participate. *Deliver us from evil!* Feel the culling process and the sense of freedom that results. Be aligned with God's will, and claim the courage granted in this petition to stand up against evil.

Evil is a difficult and elusive concept, confused by a rich and diverse history. Traditional ideas of evil have been projected into the Lord's Prayer. Some versions of the Lord's Prayer personify evil by translating the Greek phrase here as "the Evil One." Such a translation may be influenced by a tendency in Western Christianity to envision evil as Satan and the fact that the noun may be either masculine or neuter. Some have pointed out that "Satan" and "the Evil One" are Zoroastrian concepts which entered Jewish thought during the Persian period and were uncritically passed through Judaism to Christianity.

In early Old Testament times, "evil" conveyed the idea of something bad within. A rotten fig, for example, was an evil fig because something within it caused problems. "Evil" also applied to a fig not yet ripe. Anything immature and unfit for use was considered evil. The term evolved to include the errors and mistakes of people. What the word conveys today—cloak-and-dagger corruption, the flames of hell, Satan with horns and a pitchfork—robs it of its original, everyday immediacy and humanness.

We need to restore the immediacy and humanness in our understanding of evil, for this will make it something with which we can deal. As mentioned earlier, evil may be understood as the absence of God in the course of events. As such, it has several sources, a primary one being within each person's heart. To seek deliverance from evil rightly belongs here.

The Evil Within

Deliver us from evil, like the first half of this petition, is informed by James 1:13–14: "Let no one say when he is tempted, 'I am tempted by God'; for God cannot be tempted with evil and he himself tempts no one; but *each person is tempted when he is lured and enticed by his own desire*" (emphasis added). When we pray *Deliver us from evil* a big part of what we are asking of God is protection from ourselves.

In the Acts of the Apostles, there is a strange story about Simon the magician (Acts 8:9-24). Simon fascinated people with his magic tricks, leading them to believe he had a special power from God. Consequently, he had great influence on the crowds that gathered around him.

The apostle Philip entered Samaria to preach the gospel and perform miracles. Many were converted, including Simon. Peter and John then came to Samaria to pray for the coming of the Holy Spirit. Simon was impressed by the signs and wonders they were able to do, and he offered them silver if they would share the secrets of their "magic."

> Peter was quick with his rebuke: "Your silver perish with you, because you thought you could obtain the gift of God with money! You have neither part nor lot in this matter, for *your heart* is not right before God. Repent therefore of this wickedness of yours, and pray to the Lord that, if possible, *the intent of your heart* may be forgiven you" (Acts 8:20-22, emphasis added).

At first glance, the intensity of the rebuke seems out of proportion with the innocence of the request. Simon wanted something and was willing to pay for it. Wherein lies the evil? As children, are we not taught to ask for what we want and be fair about getting it? There is no violent crime here, no enticement to do wrong, no misconduct whatsoever. Simon wanted to make an honest deal. So why was Peter so stern?

The issue becomes even more confusing when we examine the temptations of Jesus in Matthew 4:1-11. After being baptized, Jesus retreated to the wilderness to be tested. The temptations of Jesus were three: (1) turn stones into bread, for he was hungry after many days of fasting, (2) cast himself down from the highest point in the temple, impressing people with his power, and (3) become a ruler of secular kingdoms. Practicality, popularity and leadership—what's wrong with these values? Are they not taught and honored in our society today? Granted the truth in Jesus' rebuttal—we are not to live by bread alone, we are not to test God, and we are to worship the one God—in what sense is practicality, social prominence, or personal ambition a temptation?

Simon's request and the temptations Jesus faced suggest that make evil a personal reality. In our own ways, we all find ourselves hungry, longing for the rocks on the desert floor to become bread. We are tempted to muster whatever power is at our disposal for our own gain.

There is nothing wrong with this, per se. Indeed, God wants us to claim our daily bread and even more. God grants us the privilege of enjoying our abundance. The evil lies in our tendency to become preoccupied with earning a living. Jesus taught this when he said to consider the birds of the air and the lilies of the field. We are to seek first God's kingdom, and our living will be provided as a matter of course (Matt. 6:25-34). Communion with God can be crowded out by our anxieties and desires within the world.

In answering his tempter, Jesus proclaimed a truth for us. We cannot live by bread alone. Our real nourishment comes from our union with God.

Likewise, with the second temptation of Jesus, which is what overcame Simon the magician, we find ourselves tempted by sensationalism. How often do we test fate by showing off, making a spectacle of ourselves, or trying to prove ourselves.

Again, there is nothing inherently wrong with this. Gain and growth come as we assert ourselves and take calculated risks. Faith demands as much. The problem comes when we rely on the power of our own ego and not on the creative power of God to manage our lives. Herein lies the evil.

Jesus answered the temptation by saying, "You shall not tempt the Lord your God." We assert ourselves for God's glory and should take no unnecessary risks for the sake of our own egos.

The third temptation of Jesus is also our own. All of us are tempted to spread our influence, to leave our mark.

As with the other temptations, there is a positive side to this. History is shaped by innovators. The problem comes, however, from the fact that each of us has a basket of fruit from the tree of the knowledge of good and evil. We love to play God by asserting our personal ideas of right and wrong, of propriety and ill manners, of how things should be and how things should not be. Given the opportunity, we would rule the kingdoms of the world according to our own standards.

Again, there is nothing wrong in assuming leadership, and what leader does not rule by what he or she feels is right? A leader cannot do otherwise. The evil lies in the subtle deception within our hearts.

Jesus warns that it is God alone whom we worship and God alone that we serve. All the kingdoms we build, all the personal standards we impose, all the influence we have on others, all are anointed only as they are sifted through God's providential plan.

When we pray *Deliver us from evil*, we seek protection not only from the evil within ourselves, but from the evil inflicted by forces outside ourselves. One of the gifts God grants us through this petition is the power of discernment, the ability to know the difference between good and evil. Often what seems like a crucifixion—evil imposing upon our lives—is a blessing in disguise. To be delivered from evil may mean yielding to a crucifixion in order to claim the blessing made possible by it.

One of the gifts from the power of discernment is knowing when to stand and challenge, and when to surrender and flow. There are times in our lives when we will be expected to confront evil, to throw the moneychangers out of the temple, so to speak. And there will be times in our lives when it is most prudent to remain silent at a trial or to welcome a crown of thorns. There are no books or formulas to tell us what is appropriate. Only the power of God within us can discern the dissonance, and we access this power by praying *Deliver us from evil*.

Praying the first part of this petition, *Leave us not in our trials*, will keep God foremost in our minds during times of testing. Praying the latter part, *Deliver us from evil*, enables us to avoid the evil inclinations of our hearts and to discern evil outside ourselves when it crowds our lives. This dual petition encourages us to trust the divine power within us and not our own strength.

Deliver us from evil! To summarize, evil is any manifestation in the world in which the consciousness behind such manifestations is self-centered, that is, lacking a universal spiritual awareness. "Deliver" means to be separated and set free from such manifestations.

That from which we are delivered sometimes arises from within ourselves. Such evil lies not necessarily in our deeds, but the tendency to become wrapped up in ourselves while performing our deeds. We are often like clams that see only to the rim of their shells. Should we open our shells and peer into the murky waters, we see only what swims or crawls through our bubble of perception. We are tempted to believe the world revolves around us and exists solely as we know it.

Part of that from which we seek deliverance is our limited perception.

Also, that from which we seek deliverance is sometimes the forces of evil that impose upon our lives from outside of ourselves, promising gifts precious for our keeping or inflicting injustices. Praying *Deliver us from evil* grants us the ability to discern such evil and either to stand and challenge or to surrender and flow.

Dear Lord, leave us not in the midst of our trials, but deliver us from evil. Having prayed thus, we complete the second cycle of petitions. We have secured our lives and with this final petition, we have cleaned our hearts of all guilt and resentment, and we have secured our path into the future. Before God, our Holy Parent—knowing, loving, and yielding to the creative source that sustains us—we now have reconciled our existence in the world in which we live.

18. The Context of the Lord's Prayer

The Lord's Prayer functions as a whole. Breaking it into parts and analyzing each phrase deepens one's understanding of the prayer. Contemplating the various petitions widens the meaning each part conveys. Praying the prayer as a unit, however, and experiencing it in context can create a spiritual presence not available when the various parts are taken separately.

In your prayer chapel, relaxed and breathing evenly, silently and slowly and meticulously repeat the entire Lord's Prayer. You may wish to repeat it several times. Pronounce each phrase as you release the air from your lungs, pausing often to sense its relationship to the whole prayer. As you pray each phrase, keep in mind its place in the twofold structure of the prayer. Throughout the experience, sense the imperative tone of the prayer and the personal relationship you have with God. Bring together all your have learned about the prayer into the experience of praying it.

Each time you pray the Lord's Prayer, add the liturgical ending *For thine is the kingdom and the power and the glory forever. Amen.* Emphasize the word *thine*. This final phrase places the prayer in its proper context, emphasizing that it is within God's realm and not your own that you pray.

I had a secretary once who took shorthand. As I dictated letters, she scratched on the tablet what looked to me like Egyptian hieroglyphics. It was remarkable to me that such writing was legible. When I asked her the meaning of a particular character, most of the time she could tell me. When she couldn't, she simply read the entire sentence and knew instantly what each character meant.

Context gives meaning to content. Background defines foreground. A white dot on a white sheet of paper is invisible because it blends with the background. A black dot on the same paper is recognized because it contrasts with the background.

The context of words shapes their significance as much as the meaning each word carries. The word "boat" means a vessel that rides on water. In the sentence, "Don't rock the boat," however, the word carries a different meaning. The word "lemon" refers to a fruit, but if you purchase an automobile and refer to it as a "lemon," the context gives the word an entirely different connotation.

Some words depend almost entirely on their context for their significance. "Green," for example, has little meaning unless you see it one something—a leaf or a blade of grass. In somewhat the same way, abstractions like "forgiveness" can be defined, but only as they are brought to bear on specific situations do they become relevant.

Any passage of scripture has a dual context: the textual and historical background within which it appears and the contemporary situation to which it speaks. Both contexts—the biblical and the modern—shape its meaning. Lifting a passage out of either context distorts its meaning and represents one of the greatest sources of error in interpreting the Bible.

The contemporary context of the Lord's Prayer has been explored in the contemplative exercises suggested in this book. When we ask for our daily bread, we become aware of the things we need. When we forgive our debtors, we remind ourselves of particular individuals who receive our forgiveness.

The textual context of the Lord's Prayer suggests the spirit with which you offer the prayer—the spirit of privacy and humility. Whether your prayers are effective depends on whether you pray with this attitude.

Consider the context of the Lord's Prayer. It appears in Matthew 6, the first verse of which sets the tone: "Beware of practicing your piety before [persons] in order to be seen by them; for then you will have no reward from your Father who is in heaven." The whole chapter contrasts practicing religion for the reputation of being religious with practicing religion for its private and personal benefits.

The first application of this principle is with giving alms. People are to sound no trumpets and are not to allow the left hand to know what the right is doing. Religion is a matter of the heart and not a script for a public performance (Matt. 6:2–4).

Before outlining the Lord's Prayer, Jesus applied this principle again to the practice of prayer. People are not to pray in front of others to make a display of it. Rather, they are to enter the privacy of their closets, shut the door, and pray in the secrecy of their own hearts. Even within these inner chambers, they are not to make a display of prayer as if trying to impress God. People are not to be flamboyant, heaping up empty phrases. God knows our needs without asking (Matt. 6:5-8).

Following the Lord's Prayer and a brief comment on forgiveness, Jesus again applies the principle, this time to fasting. While fasting, people are to avoid making a show of it. They are encouraged to disguise the practice, becoming, in a sense, spiritually invisible (Matt. 6:16-18).

The Lord's Prayer appears in the context of Jesus' teaching on humility and spiritual secrecy. Spiritual pride is subtle. For prayer to work, it must be a request for genuine communion with God, not for the enhancement of our ego-centered kingdoms.

This lesson is reflected in the Lord's Prayer itself by a constant reference to *thy* and *thine*. We pray *Hallowed be THY name.* The deception of the heart would have us standing in public places mouthing these words and really meaning, "Hallowed be our own names" or, "How majestic is our own ability."

We pray *THY kingdom come.* Our inclinations, as unconscious as it may be, is to beseech God for our own gain and the expansion of our own private theocracies.

We pray *THY will be done.* Too often, and ever so subtly, we really want our own will to be enforced.

The benediction of the Lord's Prayer echoes this theme: *For THINE is the kingdom and the power and the glory forever. Amen.* The benediction is not just a statement that happens to be true to the context of the prayer. It reiterates the context. Sincerely praying this phrase enables us to overcome the deception of our own heart, our inclination to pray for our own kingdom and power and glory while pretending to be praying for God's.

Spiritual pride is probably the biggest obstacle to overcome if we are to make the Lord's Prayer live. Accounts of people struggling with their kingdoms and power and glory occur throughout the Bible, beginning with Adam and Eve. Their temptation was to play God, the prototype of all sin.

King Saul did very little "wrong," much less than his successor, David. Yet it was David who enjoyed God's favor and who was able to overcome Saul. Saul's problem was that he stood a head taller than anyone else; he relied on his own strength rather than God's. He tried to play God over his own kingdom.

Likewise, Nebuchadnezzar was concerned with building his own kingdom and power and glory. He erected a statue to himself. Daniel's prophecy pointed to the clay feet upon which all such statues stand.

In New Testament times, the Pharisees made a similar display of their religion, praying in the synagogues and marketplaces. Jesus accused them of hypocrisy, saying they were like whitewashed tombs and like cups polished on the outside but filthy inside (Matt. 23:25-28). On one occasion, Jesus pointed to a poor widow who could afford very little. She gave all she had. By indicating that she sacrificed more than all the Pharisees combined, Jesus stressed the unpretentiousness of true spirituality (Luke 21:1-4).

Such is the context within which we pray the Lord's Prayer. The context is critical, for it makes the prayer fit with the rest of our lives. Spiritual humility is like a picture frame. People look at the picture and seldom notice the frame. Yet, it is the frame that makes the picture stand out. When we frame our prayers with secrecy and humility, our spiritual countenance stands out in ways that transcend our words.

When praying the Lord's Prayer, become "egoless," blending with the Divine Presence as a puff of smoke dissolves into the wind. Let the words *thy* and *thine*, spoken throughout the prayer, and the phrase *For thine is the kingdom and the power and the glory forever* not just remind you of God's presence. Let them draw you into God's presence.

Conclusion

We can focus our attention on two realms, the inner and the outer. To survive, we must focus our attention outward, attending to the affairs of the world in which we live. While much enjoyment is derived from this world, much stress accumulates from the opportunities and pressures it poses. We can also focus our attention inward, attending to our thoughts and feelings. Here, too, we find both enjoyment and frustration.

It is possible to go to extremes either way, pursuing and struggling with the pleasures and pressures of either our inner or outer world. People who become overly preoccupied with the outer world are intellectual types. They tend to be so involved with life, figuring things out or making ends meet or keeping relationships going that they never pause to experience their inner depths.

People who become overly preoccupied with the inner world are emotional types. They tend to retreat within, living in a dream world and being so wrapped up in their feelings that they fail to relate completely with real experiences.

These two conditions plague humanity: outer disorder and inner turmoil. People oriented outward and people oriented inward perpetually struggle with each other and within themselves to find happiness. Wherein lies inner peace and outward harmony?

Inner peace comes by periodically going beyond our thoughts and feelings, deeper into our inner worlds, and there establishing a conscious communion with God. To claim this inner peace, we must retreat from our activities in the outside world and make this journey within. Prayer, discursive or meditative, is the means by which we do this.

While prayer is the source of inner peace, inner peace is the source of outer harmony. Outer harmony comes as we bring the fruits of our inward journey to bear on the world in which we find ourselves, not necessarily in what we say, but in how we live. Indeed, our living is the extension of our prayer life. When a substantial number of persons know inner peace, the world itself will be at peace.

Prayer is a spontaneous and spiritual discipline that naturally develops our instincts for God. As a discipline, it is not tedious but a part of the joy of being Christian. It gradually intensifies a profound and sustained experience of inner peace matched by a pervasive and ever-evolving tendency for outer harmony.

Part one defined prayer as a conscious communion with God and outlined five conditions important for making an inward journey toward this communion: quiet, stillness, relaxation, natural breathing, and heightened awareness.

First, find a quiet environment. Whether on a rock beside a lake, amid the shoes of a closet, or in a private chapel, the environment should be suggestive of prayer.

Next, assume a comfortable posture that is both stable and upright. The purpose of a good posture is to foster stillness.

Then, allow your body to relax while assuming a passive attitude. Prayer means being willing, not willful.

Next, allow the breathing to settle into a slow, even, and deep rhythm. Thoughts are intimately associated with the breathing process. Calm the breathing, and the mind will also be calm.

Finally, when these conditions are in place, focus intently on your prayers, whether they be discursive or contemplative.

As you sink into prayer, adjust the climate of your inner world. To grow spiritually means to awaken. (Sleep is the biblical metaphor for a depraved human condition.) To awaken, you must give up pride, alienation, and inordinate attachments in favor of humility, forgiving love, and faith. This means dying unto yourself, an essential prerequisite for spiritual health.

Part two examined the use of the Lord's Prayer in contemplative exercises. A gestalt is included as a summary of the Lord's Prayer on p. 135.

The Lord's Prayer, a credo summary of the entire Christian message, falls into two parts. The first deals with our relationship with God; the second, with our relationship to the world in which we live.

Living the significance of the Lord's Prayer is the very essence of

Summary of the Lord's Prayer

OUR FATHER IN HEAVEN	**INVOCATION**		OUR stresses community. The parental metaphor recognizes God as our source and emphasizes our personal relationship with God. IN HEAVEN stresses the 'otherness' of God. God transcends our world.
HALLOWED BE THY NAME	**FIRST THREE PETITIONS** — Our Relationship with God — Verb Mood Is Passive	Focus on God's Creative power in the world	NAME refers to the essential nature of God. HALLOWING God's name recognizes this creative force as sacred.
THY KINGDOM COME		Focus on God's Creative power in and among us	GOD'S KINGDOM is the reign of this essential nature. To say COME invites this reign into our hearts and lives.
THY WILL BE DONE		Focus on God's Creative power through us	Once God lives in and among us, we yield our will to God's so God's creative nature finds expression through us.
ON EARTH AS IN HEAVEN	**TRANSITION**		ON EARTH AS IN HEAVEN brings the power of the first three petitions to bear on the realities we encounter in the world as recognized in the second three petitions, thus unifying the sacred and the secular.
GIVE US THIS DAY OUR DAILY BREAD	**SECOND THREE PETITIONS** — Our Relationship With the World — Verb Mood Is Active	Focus is on the Present	THIS DAY captures the immediacy of life. We live only here, only now. BREAD means all we need, here and now.
FORGIVE OUR DEBTS AS WE FORGIVE OUR DEBTORS		Focus is on the Past	All guilt is erased, granting us perpetual fresh starts, as we in turn erase our resentments toward others.
SECURITY IN OUR TRIALS DELIVER US FROM EVIL		Focus is on the Future	God does not leave us in trials, but guides us, granting strength to overcome the evil in ourselves and others.
THY KINGDOM POWER GLORY	**DOXOLOGY**		We check our pride by reminding ourselves that it is not ours, but God's kingdom, not ours but God's power, not ours but God's glory that we espouse.

TONE IS IMPERATIVE = emphatically declaring what is so, and insisting, as God's heirs, on what is rightfully ours sanctification. Developing the inner peace and outer harmony for sainthood takes time. When you pray the Lord's Prayer, search its depths and accept whatever you find.

When praying *Our Father*, be aware of the specific people and groups your include in *Our*. Sense the close, personal relationship you have with God as your heavenly Parent. When praying *who art in heaven*, realize the distance, the "otherness" of God.

When saying *Hallowed be thy name*, be aware of God's creative and sustaining power in the universe (the divine unity in all diversity) and sense this divine essence as holy. When saying *Thy kingdom come*, feel God's presence deep within yourself. Sink into the sense of inner peace that comes from being in the presence of God. When saying *Thy will be done*, surrender to the Divine Force within you. Be willing to flow with the events in your life.

Having fine-tuned your relationship with God, turn your attention to the world in which you live by pronouncing the phrase *on earth as it is in heaven*. Feel the turning, the transition, the sense of living in two realms.

When praying *Give us this day our daily bread*, call forth those things you need to sustain your life for just one day. Next, heal your personal past with the phrase *Forgive us our debts*. Continue the healing with *as we forgive our debtors*. Deliberately pronounce your forgiveness for everyone who has ever offended you. Be specific. Finally, pray *Leave us not in our trials* to bolster your courage for the future. Be aware of God's guidance through the complex maze of events that constitute your path through life. Expect that God will stay with you and give you strength during your times of testing. Intensify this petition *but deliver us from evil*, asking God to protect you from yourself—your pride, your estrangements from others, your idolatrous attachments—as well as to grant you the ability to deal with the evil that intrudes upon your life from beyond your control.

Finally, capture the overall context of the prayer with *For thine is the kingdom and the power and the glory forever. Amen.* Allow this phrase to remind you that you are not the center of the universe but that it is God's realm in which you live and move and have your being.

May God's inner peace be with you. And may your life contribute to a world in which there is good will among all people.